All that is good

THE JOURNEY TO OVERCOMING AND ACHIEVING

DR. JAMES-ETTA GOODLOE REED

All That Is Good: The Journey to Overcoming and Achieving

Author Photography
Maggie Christiansen
@maggiephotos

Book Creation and Design
DHBonner Virtual Solutions, LLC
www.dhbonner.net

ISBN for Paperback: 978-1-7362844-0-7
ISBN for eBook: 978-1-7362844-1-4

Printed in the United States of America

Dedicated to...

Mrs. Cora Pearl Woods Beach
1880 - 1962

Contents

ACHIEVING

Introduction

I HAVE LOVED READING AND writing for as long as I can remember. As a young girl, I often found myself lost in a single story of someone else's experience. At the age of eight, I wrote my first children's book; it was a simple elementary school assignment to create a story with a character. My story contained not only a character but also a counting and rhyming element. Maybe this is why Mama kept this simple little tethered book stored in a box in the back of her wardrobe.

It would take several years before discovering this second-grade treasure, but when I did, it allowed me to reflect and realize a few things. First, Mama knew I had creative talent, and that little book was proof. And second, it confirmed that I had natural writing ability, even if it took many years for me to realize it. But this realization did not start until early adulthood, back in 1995, because this was the time I intentionally purchased a journal and started actively writing and chronicling my life experiences.

Now, keep in mind I did not write every day, and it took me close to four years before I filled up that first journal; however, within that timeframe, I slowly formed the habit of writing regularly — and it was in this newly formed habit, that I noticed patterns in my behavior and my thoughts. I generally wrote when I had a negative experience, but this type of writing kept me in a dysfunctional and destructive cycle. Once I recognized this pattern, I decided to do something different, and with this decision, I began making small changes.

One small change I made was I started reading The Living Bible on a more consistent basis. And I started writing Bible verses in my journal to give me encouragement. I continued this practice when I couldn't find any words to express how I felt; I wrote Scripture to provide me with hope. Who knew that this simple practice of putting my feelings on paper and writing Bible verses would put me on a path to clarity, healing, and happiness. I believe healing begins when you find your voice.

Nevertheless, writing my feelings was one thing, and writing Scriptures was a good start, but examining my life through self-reflection was a whole different ball game. But the skills to analyze and evaluate to make meaning from my experiences did not happen until I was in graduate school to earn a degree in adult and continuing education. It was there that I used all the rich qualitative data I had collected about myself in those journals to dig deeper into adult development and the role of reflection for cultural identity. And that trip through my journals took me on a transformational journey of a lifetime. But it was my willingness to live my life twice, through reflection, that I was able to learn and unlearn so much about myself.

Romans 8:28 says that all things work together for good . . . not some, but ALL. When I honestly looked back over my life, I saw that everything led me to where I needed to be because everything that happened to me was a reflection of what was going on inside me.

Like the stories of First Lady Michelle Obama and Madam Vice President Kamala Harris, I start my story by reflecting on my childhood: how I was raised, who raised me, and the environment that I was raised in. I had a stable home life and a really good childhood, even if it was not ideal. My biological mother moved away when I was a toddler, and around this same time, my biological father was murdered; therefore, I was raised by my maternal great-grandparents, who I affectionately called Mama and Daddy. So it was my multi-generational upbringing that set me on the path of stabled values like faith, family, and education. But growing up, I did not like school.

It is common practice in the Black community for children to be raised by extended family members, and studies show that children who experience life with absent biological parents drop out of high school, with 40% being Black female students. This could have easily been me because I hated everything about my K-12 experience and was never interested in college. But my life experience and writing about those experiences slowly became the bridge that would lead me to have a passion for education — and my journals, filled with lots of hills and valleys, became my roadmap to this discovery. My journals helped me to uncover patterns in my behavior like hiding or denying my emotions, questioning my reality, or performing to seek approval from others.

I spent years in this destructive cycle, and without writing in my journals and reflecting on my experiences, I would've been completely unaware of how I accepted shame and low self-worth as a way of life, which kept me depressed and disconnected from my authentic self. Journal writing became my tool to value feeling good — and life is meant to feel good *to* you and be good *for* you.

The beginning of each chapter starts with a Bible verse that encouraged me, with my first journal entry showing up in chapter 5. From that point forward, I continue to share my innermost thoughts and how I felt as I had the experience in its raw and candid form. At the end of the book, you will find a QR Code to scan, and it will take you to pictures and videos that go along with my story. Although I use very few specific names, the details of an event are how I viewed them and what I experienced when it happened. I make no apologies, but I have made peace, which is why I've decided to share my story with the world. It is my story told by me. I hope it enlightens you. I pray it inspires you to never give up.

The QR Code also provides resources and prompts so that you can capture those small bits of data about yourself. Your life experiences are valuable, and it all helps to shape who you are becoming. Because true power unfolds when you can look back, appreciate, and embrace *All That is Good!*

Living

CHAPTER 1

Good Start

> "Trust in the Lord instead. Be kind and good to others; then you
> will live safely here in the land and prosper, feeding in safety."
> *-Psalm 37:3*

KENTUCKY. OFTEN KNOWN AS a border state, but with strong ties to the South due to its agricultural and economic development. Kentucky. The place of Cassius Clay, Muhammed Ali and bell hooks. Kentucky. The place of corn, tobacco, bourbon, horses and hemp. Kentucky, good land, good living and good people. Meanwhile, Kentucky was a state that did not officially adopt the Thirteenth Amendment until 1976. I was born in 1971.

I grew up thirty miles east of Louisville in a small farming community where it was not uncommon to have traffic halted to a snarl because a tractor slowly made its way down the road. And like most communities of its time, there was an invisible line to divide the Black families from the White families — the haves and the have not's. My rural, segregated community had an iron bridge named

"Who'd' A Thot It," which sat over a creek in a semi-wooded area, directly across from the county jail not far from the center of town. Every community story has two versions that circulate, a white version and a Black version. The white version of "Who'd A Thot It" bridge was that it got its name because a little house was precariously built just above the creek on the side of a hill, and "Who'da thot to build a house there?" The Black version of the bridge went like this, "Who'da thot they hung so many niggers there?"

Henry Clay Street was a street reserved for mostly Black families and Black-owned businesses. This street was wedged right in between the invisible line that separated Black from white. The block where I lived contained single-family homes and an independent living facility for adults with disabilities. Further down the street were a Black-owned funeral home, a Black-owned barbershop, and two Black churches. It was a good area that was safe to play outside and sit on the front porch. Clay Street was a good street and a good place for me to start. It was common to see residents from the assisted living facility aimlessly wander and walk past the house where I lived.

As a child, I never noticed anything different about any of them. What I saw was a young man or woman walk down the street who occasionally had a loud conversation, even if it appeared that no one else was around. It wasn't strange. It was just part of the fabric of my environment. A lot of talent and success came from Clay Street, and everybody was kind to one another.

For the most part, Clay Street was an area reserved for Black, middle-class, working families who were educated beyond high school. The houses varied in sizes and shapes, from duplexes to bi-levels with front porches and back yards. Behind Clay Street were several other streets with large tri-level homes occupied mostly by those who worked in education or other noble occupations. The residents on that side of the street were predominately White, with the handful of Black families and what I classified as elite, upper working class. Meanwhile, a small family-owned grocery store sat between these two sections of my neighborhood and separated the Black middle working-class from the Black elite upper working-class. As a child, I bounced in and out of that little grocery store on a regular basis, especially when I was sent to get a package of Kool cigarettes for Daddy Boots. He would give me a dollar for the pack of Kool, and if I had a quarter left over, I bought a piece of candy or a slice of Dixie Loaf lunchmeat.

Clay Street also contained a large tobacco warehouse. This large tobacco warehouse stretched from Clay Street and curved around the block to take up part of another street. Tobacco production was big business in my small county, and this warehouse stayed busy, especially at certain times of the year. Tobacco season made Clay Street a flurry of activity with familiar faces and those faces that only came around for seasonal work.

The house where I grew up was modest in structure compared to the surrounding homes, and our house sat directly beside the tobacco warehouse. Although our house was significantly smaller in comparison to others on the street, our house had the most people living under its roof. Mama Pauline and Daddy Boots were poor, working-class farmers with a combined 8th-grade education who valued their faith and their family. Even after they moved from the sharecropper farm where they each grew up and moved ten miles into "town" when they purchased the house, they brought chickens, a rooster, built a coop, and planted a small garden in the backyard so they would always have a way to feed their family. Imagine a young, Black couple with the opportunity to live in one of the most prominent areas for Black families, and they bring their own farm animals. They were the only ones on that street with their own personalized farmer's market.

But, owning a house on Clay Street was a huge accomplishment that carried significant symbolism and wealth for Mama Pauline and Daddy Boots, even if they had not built their house to offer privacy to a multi-generational household. At one point, they had up to 15 or more people living under its roof at one time. Often a curtain or bed sheet was the only privacy to separate one room from the other. Later, but before I was born, Daddy built a room on the back of the house, just past the kitchen. This room was the designated "boys" room with two sets of bunk beds on either side.

The "boys" room stayed hot in the summer and cold in the winter because insulation was not very good throughout the house in general. There was no central heating/cooling system, so they used plastic to cover all of the windows throughout the house to keep cold air out in the winter. A huge pot belly electric stove sat in the center for heat while box fans were placed in every window for coolness. In the meantime, the bedroom in the front of the house was the designated "girls" room. This room contained one queen size bed, an oversized dresser, and a wardrobe. Mama and Daddy's room was right in the center of the house, with the one and only bathroom directly beside their room.

To get to the bathroom, you had to walk through Mama and Daddy's room. The small bathroom had the necessary amenities for indoor plumbing (sink and toilet), which was a blessing, but it had no shower, only a clawfoot tub. If the faucet were not left to drip in the winter, the pipes would freeze, and then water would need to be carried from a neighboring house for us to bathe and flush the toilet. A large teakettle was kept on the potbelly stove to provide hot water when this happened. But regardless of any potential plumbing issue, there was never a time that the house was not bustling with people and food. And in those early days, that house was a house filled with love, laughter, and lots of stories.

Throughout the week, we ate supper at 5 p.m. when Daddy Boots came home from work. And every Saturday, we went to Winn Dixie to buy groceries for the week. Sunday dinner was prepped Saturday night. Sunday dinner was a big deal at that little house, especially if there was a guest at the table. One time, the church pastor came over for dinner, which was not uncommon since Daddy Boots was a deacon and the church was just a few blocks away. We all gathered around the table, prayed, and passed around the platters of hot, delicious tender roast beef with potatoes, fresh garden green beans, sweet corn pudding, and sliced vine-ripened tomatoes.

As conversations were being had, the television, which was in the same room as the dining room table, played a familiar commercial. I squirmed in my seat as an eager six-year-old eating my plate of food without realizing that I had started humming the jingle to the commercial. Daddy Boots shot me a stern look, and Mama's voice was low and direct as she told me to "Stop it"! Apparently, it was not polite to sing and dance at the dinner table, especially with Pastor Taylor sitting there. So yeah, Sunday dinner was a big deal in that little house.

One look at the family tree reveals Mama Pauline and Daddy Boots as my maternal Great-grandparents, but they were the parents who took care of me from infancy to adulthood, so by every account, they were my Mama and Daddy. Looking back, I realize that I had a good upbringing; though it was not ideal, it was still good.

My biological mother, Cookie, was the oldest of six children and the oldest grandchild of Mama Pauline and Daddy Boots. Cookie and her mother, Ann, never had a close, loving relationship. As the story goes, after Cookie's parents got divorced, her father took up a relationship with another woman. This other woman was "sweet and kind" to Cookie, which only forged a deeper wedge between Cookie and her mother. So, Cookie spent a lot of time with her grandmother, Mama Pauline.

Cookie was a beautiful brown skin, bright-eyed young girl with long braids down her back who dreamed of being a model. Not only was she beautiful, but she was also brilliant in school and stood out among her peers. However, these attractive attributes and high functioning skills often became the object of negative attention and bullying at school. Once, someone pulled Cookies' long braids so hard that it caused her nose to bleed, and Mama Pauline had to come to get her from school. The bullying continued and intensified once she became a teenager in high school, but by this time, she had found a way to cope by skipping school and smoking behind the school building. The excessive absence from school and behavior was reported to Mama Pauline, and Cookie was suspended from school as a consequence. After this incident, Cookie never returned to school and instead dropped out her junior year.

My grandmother, Ann, was a kaleidoscope of a woman. She was the oldest of four and a born leader who was extremely smart. She attended Lincoln Institute, an all-Black boarding high school in Shelby County, Kentucky. Ann had experience in teaching, nursing, and culinary. She was often sought after for her culinary skills by prominent White families in the community. And her hot-water cornbread was the talk of the town. Ann was funny, creative, and an avid reader who loved all kinds of books.

Additionally, she was a gifted writer who kept notebooks of poems and various other writings. But Ann also had another side that was quick-tempered and rigid. When triggered, her tone of voice would slice straight to the white meat and leave deep scar tissue. She battled depression most of her adult life and experienced extreme highs and lows, resulting in extended stays at a medical facility to get treatment. Her ability to parent her oldest daughter, Cookie, went through a series of its own highs and lows.

As a young teen, Cookie worked odd-and-end jobs, but opportunities were scarce without a high school diploma. And to deepen the gap between Cookie and her mother, an event happened when Cookie was a teen that I don't think either one ever healed from.

One day, Cookie was on a lunch break and went to her mother's house for something to eat. No one was home, so she helped herself to the last pieces of bologna and made a sandwich. When her mother came home, the man she lived with got upset because there was no more bologna for him to make a sandwich for his lunch. With this, Cookies' mother became enraged and demanded to know who the hell had been in her house when she was not home and ate up all the damn food. Cookie gave in to the pressure of the interrogation and admitted to her mother, "Hell yes, I ate the bologna. So what?" This response set emotions to an all-time high, and Cookie was slapped in the face by her mother because she ate the last bologna sandwich. Unfortunately, the pattern of dysfunction and hurt only grew between Cookie and her mother through the years.

Cookie eventually moved away from Kentucky when I was around two years old. Tobacco was big business in my small town. She worked at the tobacco warehouse, and when the seasonal workers returned to North Carolina to continue working until the cycle brought them back to Kentucky to work in tobacco again, she went with them with the understanding that once she got on her feet, she would come back and get me. When Cookie got somewhat on her feet, she returned to Kentucky to take me with her to North Carolina. Still, Daddy Boots said "No," and she returned to North Carolina, where she continued to live — only returning to Kentucky to visit each year.

While living in North Carolina, Cookie became pregnant again, and this time gave birth to a set of twin girls. Unfortunately, one of the twins died of sudden infant death syndrome weeks after delivery. I was around six years old at the time, and there was so much that I did not understand. I remember a group of us piled into Daddy Boots Chevy Impala and made the road trip to North Carolina for the funeral. The energy was so sad and dark. Everybody cried, and Cookie stayed in bed most of the time. Mama Pauline and Daddy Boots decided that they would take care of this new infant who just lost her identical twin since they were already taking care of me. So, we brought the surviving twin back to Kentucky with us so she and I could grow up together, and that infant baby cried a lot. And the only thing I knew for sure, I was a big sister.

In the meantime, I've come to learn this about Cookie, my biological mother and James, my biological father, and the relationship they had, which resulted in the creation of me.

James was in his late 30's and Cookie in her early 20's when they met. He was from Louisville, a tall, dark, handsome muscular hustler-type who frequented the small town where Cookie lived. He came to hang out with the locals, shoot craps, and play cards at the gambling house on the weekends. James was a nice man, but a beast in the streets if you crossed him, and a fierce protector of his family. Somewhere in my father's life, he served time in prison for a robbery. Also, James was married with children before taking up with another woman, eventually leaving the other woman after meeting Cookie to share a house together in Louisville.

James played an active role in his relationship with Cookie while she was pregnant with me by working and providing for her. He was even at the hospital when I was born. The story goes, Cookie went into labor on a hot night in late September, and James rushed her to St. Joseph Hospital and told the staff, "My wife is having a baby." His announcement was a big deal because he and Cookie were not legally married. But when Cookie woke from her twilight sleep, she found James asleep in a chair beside her bed with pink hair rollers in his hair wrapped in a scarf because he was known to wear his hair pressed and curled. James insisted on naming me after him, and they agreed on the name James Etta.

At this time, my half-brother, with whom I share the same father, was about 14 years old. Although he lived in the house with James and Cookie when I was born, he spent his teenage years on a path to juvenile delinquency, in and out of detention centers. By the time my brother reached adulthood, he had committed various crimes with the most serious charge of manslaughter and is currently serving a life sentence in a minimum-security federal prison. We recently started to communicate, and through our communication, I've learned the history of violence on my father's side of the family. It seemed like the only way to resolve an issue was through behavior that involved physical force with the intent to hurt, damage, or kill.

Subsequently, in March 1975, James, my biological father, was shot in the back eight times and died on the streets of Baltimore — he was 42 years old. James had no identification on him when he was murdered, so it took a while for his next of kin to be notified, which was the wife he was separated from but never legally divorced. It should be noted that the relationship between James and Cookie had ended before he was killed; therefore, growing up, I never knew my biological father and only recently learned the above information through archival research, stories, and reflections. Nobody ever directly talked to me about James, and as I got older, I became more curious as to who this man was who I was named after but had no information about. Whenever I asked about him, my inquiry was usually met with deflection, denial, or blatant, "Some things are better off not knowing."

But through my pursuit of the truth and my natural desire to research for deeper understanding, I have come to know the circumstances surrounding my issues with abandonment, grief, and rejection. Nevertheless, I have an older sister and brother, with whom I share the same father, and a younger sister, with whom I share the same mother. But for six years, I was the youngest child who lived in my multi-generational household full time. Yes, there were older relatives who lived there who had children, but they were in and out depending on their particular situation.

Mama Pauline had an open-door policy, so the small green-colored house with aluminum siding on Clay Street was home to all of her family. But my situation was a bit different; I was a permanent resident until my little sister came along.

When Cookie came to visit for the holidays or summer break, she stayed there too. So, sleeping two, three, or more to a bed was the norm, and making a pallet on the floor to have a place to sleep was not unusual. Neither was sharing bathwater or washing underwear in the sink and hanging up to dry overnight to have clean underwear available. We did not have a washer and dryer and only made monthly trips to the laundromat — we were the family who took up all the washers and all the dryers.

At the time, I did not realize that these conditions were signs of poverty. But even under those circumstances, I never went without anything. I was always clean, decent, and a high value was placed on faith, family, and education. I was loved, protected, and nurtured, which was what I needed to have a good start.

CHAPTER 2

Good Education

"The Lord is good. When trouble comes he is the place to go!
And he knows everyone who trusts in him!" *-Nahum 1:7*

I WAS AN EAGER LEARNER at an early age and excited about school even after I had an incident in first grade where a teacher embarrassed me in front of the class. Without any awareness, I developed a bias against teachers who looked like my first-grade teacher, a White female. By the time I got to fourth grade, my interest in school quickly started to fade because that is when the bullying started.

While I played the violin in fourth grade, in fifth grade, I played the clarinet. I should use the term "tried" because I never became very good at either of these instruments. In the meantime, practice was held after school, in the music room that was in a separate building across from the secondary school. I could not read music, but I could understand the pattern of the colors that coded the melody to be played. About the second or third week of practice, the mean girls waited across the street for me to walk home after practice. At first, I was clueless as to why they were there. Although they lived within walking distance of the school — they lived in the opposite direction of where I lived, so why were they still hanging around the school an hour after school was dismissed?

One day, they greeted me with smiles as I lugged my backpack on my shoulder and carried my violin headed towards Clay Street. As I got closer, their smiles turned to sneers as they yelled mean things to me. "You THINK you're cute." "You trying to be White." "I will beat you up." "You bet not be at school tomorrow, or we will beat you up." "You are fat and ugly." "I will smack your glasses off." The faster I walked, the more they crowded on my heels, shouting these hurtful things at me.

I finally crossed over Washington Street and quick-walked to the corner of Main Street, and then crossed my way to get closer to Clay Street. Once I reached Clay Street, I glanced over my shoulder to see that the mob of mean girls had stopped at the corner of Washington Street. It was as if their meanness could not cross over into all the goodness that Clay Street had to offer. As long as I could make it to Clay Street, they could not get me. Clay Street provided a protective barrier for me; I was safe and sound until I returned to school the next day.

On another day, after school, I was at home, and someone I knew knocked on my door and asked if I could come outside and play. I thought it odd that she would be at my door since she did not live on Clay Street. But I trusted her and thought this would be a chance for me to make a friend. I yelled through the house to let Mama know that I would be outside playing and gleefully followed my new friend down the street and around the corner. Little did I know that it was a setup because the entire group of mean-girl-bullies was waiting for me when I got around the corner.

They circled me and started pushing me back and forth between them and shouting hurtful things at me. I tried to press my way through the group and run back to my house, but I couldn't — they had me surrounded.

The first punch landed on the top of my right arm, and as I grabbed it to make sure that it was still attached to my body, the second punch came to my left arm, and then more punches to the body. I just balled up and tried to protect my face and head. Mama, who had an eye and ear to the street, suspected that something was not right when she saw me walk down the street with my new friend. Mama had been standing on the street in front of our house, waiting for me to come back home or to see me playing with my new friend.

Instead, Mama heard the commotion coming from around the corner and walked down to investigate. At the sight of Mama standing with her hand on her hip, staring down each bully eyeball to eyeball, the crowd scattered. Each made haste and got across the street and back to their side of town. Mama yelled out threats to leave me alone and not to ever come that way again. The next day at school, I was teased for getting beat up and for my Mama coming to rescue me.

In middle school, the bullying transitioned into peer pressure, especially when it came to hooking up with boys. In eighth grade, I was in a talent show with three other girls. We performed "In My House" by the Mary Jane Girls. A somewhat provocative song and performance now that I think about it, but at the time, it was purely for fun. The four of us stayed after school to practice our choreographed routine in the auditorium. So, there was no secret that we would perform in the talent show. However, when the day came, the reaction from the crowd was mixed. The teachers and principal all stood around with their eyes wide in shock and awe of our dance moves.

Meanwhile, the pre-teen boys all cheered for the same reason and because our costumes resembled the outfits worn by the group in the music video: a mid-drift shirt, skintight stirrup style leggings, and mini skirt. I was in that awkward stage of development, and it was the first time anyone saw me without my usual oversized clothes. I was generally teased about having a big head, large nose, or big feet, but this time the attention was on my hips and butt.

Not long after my Apollo performance as a Mary Jane Girl, rumors started to spread around school about a boy who liked me. And for the sake of this story, let's call him Bullwinkle. He played several sports and was very popular, so everybody knew him and was friends with him. Then one day, a girl I knew convinced me to hang out with her after school. When we got to the hangout spot, Bullwinkle was there along with his friend Rocky. I immediately knew what was expected to come next since Rocky and the girl who was with me were known to be dating and having sex. When the two of them walked off together, I was left alone with Bullwinkle. He started smiling and coming close to me, eyeballing me up and down, talking about how good I looked with those tight leggings on in the talent show. I froze, not knowing what to do. He continued to bump and grind against me with this stupid grin on his face the whole time. He then took my hand and put it on his bulging crotch.

Again, I froze. Before I knew it, his pants were unzipped, his penis stood at attention, and he continued to grind up against me. He gyrated, huffed, puffed, and breathed his hot breath on my neck. I just stood there frozen. Rocky and his girl reappeared, having finished what they both came to do. Bullwinkle quickly backed away from me, zipped up his pants, and ran off with Rocky while the girl who was with me and I ran in the opposite direction. Everybody laughed, but me. At school, the next day, rumors spread that Bullwinkle and I had 'did it.' It was a lie, and I denied the allegation, but it only made matters worse. After that, I found it hard to trust people and struggled with friendships. But there was one person who was worthy of my trust and became a really good friend.

Allison lived around the corner from Clay Street, which was exclusive for what some might consider elite, educated Black families. Her father was a high school science teacher and basketball coach. He broke several barriers by being the first Black man to serve on several state education agency committees. He was a pillar in the community and a strong advocate for education, especially for Black students. Allison's house stood head and shoulders above the small overcrowded place where I lived. Her home had three levels, a screened-in porch, and a fenced backyard. She shared a room with her sister, and they each had their own bed — unlike me, who shared a queen size bed with several other female relatives.

Allison and I became fast friends. Our last name began with the same letter, so we were always in the same homeroom class. We attended the same church and joined the choir, junior usher, and Sunday school class together. We even got baptized on the same Sunday. Allison and I were the same age and our birthdays were just weeks apart. We walked to school together, and it was on those walks that Allison often led the conversation and talked about college, graduate school, New York, and Paris. Allison had a global, forward-thinking mindset and talked about things that I didn't know existed. The only Jaguar I knew was the exotic animal I briefly remembered from a page in National Geographic.

When Allison talked about Jaguar, she spoke about the type of luxury vehicle she would drive after she finished college. We were adolescents in middle school, and she knew exactly where she would attend college. Allison introduced me to Nikki Giovanni, Maya Angelou, and James Baldwin. She was a walking encyclopedia but not overbearing or in-your-face with what she knew, and she was down-to-earth, loving, and very funny. She was a good person with a good heart — a good friend. Where we might have been different in our mindsets about education, we were similar in our love for family, faith, and friendship.

Education was ranked high in my family's value system. As a child, I always saw Mama Pauline reading and writing. She thrived in learning new things. She held intellectual conversations with anyone who had the privilege of sitting at the dining room table; whether speaking with the pastor, the neighbor, the insurance salesman, the farmer, or the mail carrier, she had wisdom and knowledge to impart. I always viewed her as a smart and wise woman. Keep in mind, her formal education stopped at eighth grade, but Mama Pauline's informal learning continued until just before she died. Regularly, she completed word-seek and crossword puzzles to keep her mind sharp. Whenever I needed help spelling a word, she was my dictionary. The Holy Bible and Reader's Digest were just some of her daily reading companions.

Before I was old enough to go to school, she read some of her favorite Scriptures to me, and once I began going to Sunday school, I came to understand the Bible stories Mama told me. When I complained about school, Mama always reminded me what a privilege it was to get a "good education," and that knowledge was something no one could take away from me.

In the meantime, all through high school, my only goal after graduation was to get as far away from Kentucky as possible. I had no plans to attend college. There were not many family members in my multi-generational household who had completed college. Of those who did, they encountered significant life events along the way, like teenage pregnancy, marriage, jobs, etc. I do not ever remember having anyone clearly explain what a 'good education' looked like or show me the steps I needed to take to obtain a good education beyond high school. The reason for my urgency to escape Kentucky was because of my horrible K-12 experience of being labeled an "at-risk" student because of my low-test scores, low academic achievement, school suspensions, and behavioral issues.

Additionally, I was bullied and even teased for being gay because I hung out with one particular girl a lot. I hated everything about my small town. I hated everything about my school environment.

In high school, I had two fights. The first fight happened directly after lunch one day. I had had enough of the name-calling and shaming, and when the bully approached and hit me, I hit back. The next thing I knew, we were being pulled apart and hauled off to the assistant principal's office. I was suspended from school for three days. When Mama Pauline and Daddy Boots came to pick me up from school, Mama looked at me and simply said, "Puddin, we did not raise you like this. You know better than to behave this way." All I could do was cry because she was right.

Nevertheless, the second fight happened later that same school year after a basketball homecoming game. I happened to be nominated for homecoming queen, Allison was nominated too, and it was after the halftime event that I found myself in another fight with a different bully right outside the girl's bathroom. My entire family was there sitting in the stands. When word spread that I was in the hallway fighting, Mama once again gave me her speech about how I should know better. She was disappointed that I did not walk away from the nonsense. I was disappointed too but did not know where to turn for positive reinforcement and guidance. Instead, I coped with the hell I found myself in through underage drinking, drugs, and sex.

I had a lot of freedom growing up. But all that freedom felt like abandonment to me, especially when it came to hanging out with friends, so at age 15, I had my first encounter with the police. I was a passenger, joyriding in a stolen car with open wine coolers. The officer took us to the jail and called our parents to pick us up. This could be viewed as a slap on the wrist or a small-town tactic due in part to the reality that the officer recognized the driver because she was a White girl and he knew her father — a well-known figure in the community — so the police officer was familiar with her late-night cruising activity. But this time, she had passengers, and we were Black. However, after I gave my home address, the officer realized where I lived on Clay Street because it was located just blocks from the police station. Even if the police officer did not know my family personally like he knew the White teen driver's family, he was aware of the caliber of Black families that lived on Clay Street, which somehow made a difference.

Needless to say, this incident was a massive disappointment to Mama Pauline and Daddy Boots. It was the late 1980's, and even without modern technology, it wasn't uncommon for residents in my rural community to have police scanners in their homes to keep up on the local happenings.

Once the call came across the scanner about a group of teens joyriding with alcohol, rumors spread like wildfire throughout my small town about our run-in with the police. This incident happened on a school night, and by the time I got to school the next day, everybody in the entire building already knew and teased me about being in "jail without the bail." I was trending before Twitter was even invented. I hated everything about my life at that time and hated my small town even more. I did not have the tools to stand up for myself. I did not know how to make it all stop or not let it bother me. I was vulnerable and ignorant and fell deep into all the manipulation that peer pressure brought on in an effort to fit in to try and make the bullying stop. It didn't.

I lost my virginity to a knucklehead who was older and way more experienced than me. One summer night, I had sex with him on the cold, wet ground behind one of the houses. It was quick, awkward, painful, and humiliating. After it was over, I limped home with what felt like water running down my leg. I quickly ran through the house to the bathroom and discovered that it was not water; it was blood. I had started my period. I was never fully informed about my menstrual cycle and unclear about what to do. I yelled out for Mama Pauline to come and help me. Mama entered the bathroom and found my bloody underwear and pants on the floor. She calmly told me that my period had started, then gathered some old rags, ripped them apart, and instructed me to wash up, get a clean pair of underwear and place clean rags inside my underwear until somebody went to the store and bought a box of Kotex.

I stayed in the house, confined to the bed for about a week. Once I returned to the group of unsupervised teens I hung out with, they drank bourbon and smoked cigarettes, so I followed the group and started drinking and smoking too and tried to fit in. The older boy who I gave my virginity to still hung around me, so we started having sex all the time any place that we could – abandoned houses, apartment complex laundry room, outdoors in the woods. It didn't matter when or where . . . we had sex all the time. I craved the attention and got used to having sex; I became good at it. I knew it. He knew it. Everybody knew it.

It was only by the grace of God that I did not have multiple pregnancies as a young teen. I was a hot mess. I was a juvenile delinquent with a lot of freedom, minimal guidance and lived up to every negative label placed on me.

Where I had a lot of freedom at 15, Allison used wisdom in her decision-making when it came time to hanging out as a teenager. I convinced Allison to go to junior prom because she did not date any of the boys in school, mainly because her father worked at the high school and nobody wanted to get on his bad side. And when it came time to attend the prom, she and I made a pact that we would double date and look out for each other, so neither one of us was taken advantage of at the end of the night. I knew Allison was not into what I was into. I respected her. When I hung around Allison, there was no pressure to be anything but myself, and I valued that about our friendship. We went to our Junior prom with a set of brothers, who also happened to be our friends, and we all had a lot of fun that night. Allison and I decided to go without any dates for senior prom and had the best time in our fancy outfits hanging around all of our friends.

Senior year of high school came fast. My graduating class contained 214 students. The night of graduation, Allison and I sat beside each other. We knew that all of those years living and learning from each other were about to change. We were headed in two different directions, and as we walked out of the gymnasium, silent tears streamed down our cheeks. We gripped hands and walked side by side: no words, just love, admiration, and appreciation for each other. Somehow, before we made our exit out into the world and left the gymnasium, we looked up to the stands and flashed a smile for the camera. We smiled for the memories made and dreams shared. We smiled for our bond and our friendship.

Consequently, my errant behavior inside and outside of school led me to believe that I did not have what it took to succeed in college. Therefore, I made no plans to attend. My only goal was to escape the cycle of hell I created for myself in Kentucky. So the day after I graduated high school, I packed my bag and piled in the car with relatives who attended my graduation and moved to Dallas, Texas. Immediately I started to work as a cashier in the bookstore of the newly opened Sixth Floor Museum. I also enrolled in the local community college yet never attended class. Not soon after I moved to Texas, I started to date a guy, which was my pattern. I never had trouble finding a boyfriend. I knew what any boy wanted and freely gave it away. It did not matter if he had other girls; if he gave me any attention, I jumped in with both feet.

Early fall 1989, I turned 18 at the end of September, and by mid-October, I moved out of the house with my relatives and moved into an apartment with my new boyfriend. I was young and reckless, so exceptionally reckless, living my life entirely on the edge. I did not care what anybody had to say. I did what I wanted to do. I moved in with a guy I barely knew, in an empty apartment, with only a mattress on the floor, halfway across town. I was in a big city with a small-town mindset. I was in over my head without any clue as to how to get out. I was a country bumpkin without a hint as to how to handle the city slicker I found myself entangled with. But just a few months after I moved in with him, my job at the bookstore ended. New management came in and required all employees to have a minimum of a four-year degree to continue working at the museum.

I was out of a job. I tried to find employment elsewhere and quickly learned how difficult it was with only a high school diploma and no car. It did not take long for my unstable relationship with my boyfriend to turn troublesome. The abuse started early on, but I ignored his threats and continued to see him. He had several other girlfriends while he dated me. Even after we moved in together, his bad behavior did not stop.

One time I became sick . . . like doubled over with level ten pain in my lower abdomen. He drove me to the doctor's office and dropped me off while he cruised around in this red low-rider truck and would swing back around to pick me up when he thought I was finished. I was completely at his disposal, and he knew it. The doctor was an African female with a thick Nigerian accent. This was a first for me because I grew up where there were only White doctors. It was hard for me to get comfortable from the physical pain and where I was seeing a Black female doctor for the first time. Not to mention that I was over the age of 18, and it was my first time at a doctor's visit without Mama. I was scared. I needed Mama Pauline.

After the examination, the look on the doctor's face told me the news was not good. But before she gave me any information, she asked me a series of questions like, where was I from, how long had I been in Texas, and who did I live with? One of her final questions was, "What were my plans for the future?" I answered all of her questions and gave an honest answer about not having any plans. And then she said, "Whoever this guy is that you live with must not care anything about you because if he did, he would not treat you the way he does or put you at risk."

I was diagnosed with acute pelvic inflammatory disease. The doctor prescribed several high-powered antibiotics with orders to rest. I left the office in tears and waited outside until I heard the booming system of the red low-rider truck coming back to pick me up. I explained what the doctor said and how I needed rest; he announced that he had to take care of something before taking me home. I ended up spending the next six hours waiting for him while he got a bumper repaired and repainted on his truck.

The routine became that we fought, I left our apartment and went to my relative's house, he showed up with gifts, flowers, and an apology, and I moved back in with him. I had no job and no income. I became utterly dependent on him. By this time, I graduated from small-town bourbon and weed, I was strung out and turned out. I was weak-minded and used heavy drugs on a regular basis to numb my pain.

Things turned horribly one night, so horrible that I could not see my way out of the hell I was in. I felt insecure, alone, and hopeless. This was the night that I hit rock bottom, and I attempted suicide. All I wanted was someone to listen and understand, but I did not have the tools to communicate what I needed or who I needed it from, so my suicide attempt was a cry for help, not to end my life. I am glad that I did not die that night.

Eventually, I broke away from my toxic relationship with my abusive boyfriend and moved back in with my relatives. But Texas wasn't all bad because I learned how to ride a transit bus in a metropolitan city. I grew to appreciate the historical celebration of Juneteenth, and I fell absolutely in love with chicken fried steak. Nevertheless, the reality of life in Texas became harder and harder for me to withstand, and after a year, I ultimately returned home to Kentucky.

Learning

CHAPTER 3

Good Friend

> "...But men who encourage the upright to do good shall be given a worthwhile reward." -*Proverbs 28:10*

I FOUGHT A LOT OF inner turmoil and tried to figure out what to do next once I returned to Kentucky after a year in Texas. With no direction for putting my broken life back together, I turned to my good friend Allison. Her father had a lot of influence in the community, and he advocated for all children, especially Black children, to have opportunities to learn new things that they would otherwise not have. One Sunday, Allison's father approached me after church and inquired about my plans for the future. I told him that I was unsure of what to do. He asked, "You can answer a phone and take a message, can't you?" "Yes, sir," I replied.

Next, he instructed me to meet him at the Kentucky Department for Employment Services the next day at 8 a.m. sharp. There was a small satellite office in our area, and I worked as a summer student employee answering the phones. It was my first office job.

Meanwhile, Allison had just completed her first semester of college and encouraged me to enroll at the same university she attended in the fall. I did not think I was good enough to go to college. But Allison's enthusiasm about learning stuck with me.

So, with Allison's encouragement and advice, I applied and was accepted into Western Kentucky University. In August 1990, at 19, I packed my bags again and, this time, headed off to college. I had no clue what my major would be or how I would pass any of the college classes, but I knew that if things did not work out, I was only a two-hour car ride from home and not a 22-hour Trailway bus ride. College gave me a second chance, and this time I would not make the same mistakes I made in Texas. Or so I thought.

I moved into the same dorm where Allison lived, close to my classes but without air-conditioning. Although it was the beginning of the fall semester, Kentucky had several weeks of scorching hot, humid weather before it got cooler. Two weeks after the semester started, I met a girl in one of my classes, and she lived in an air-conditioned dorm. Her roommate never showed up. The two of us completed the roommate request form and were approved for me to move into her dorm room. I got a good break, quickly loaded all my belongings on a grocery cart, and moved across campus to cooler quarters. My roommate and I set up our room to look like a mini-apartment, and we partied in that room like we didn't live on campus. Most of my new friends lived off-campus because they were from the local community. The first football homecoming weekend, I had 15-20 people partying in my dorm room. It's not a wonder that I did not get expelled from the university for violating the school's alcohol policy in a campus residence hall.

In my new dorm, I met a few girls. I formed friendships with the girls and soon discovered that my new roommate and I had a lot in common. We both liked to drink, smoke, and party. In my mind, it was the best of all worlds: I lived on my own – well, sort of, on a college campus, and no one told me what to do, and I had friends who liked the same things that I did. I filled my first semester with hook-ups, beer pongs, and weed bongs. I made a lot of bad decisions. The only difference between Texas and campus was that if I had to return home, I wouldn't have so far to travel.

Although my perspective would eventually start to change at the end of my first semester, in the beginning, I enjoyed every ounce of freedom I had at Western Kentucky University. With my low-performance scores in high school, I took a lot of remedial classes in my first year.

Still, I somehow completed that first semester, but I received several pieces of bad news when Christmas break came. First, one of the friends who lived in my dorm lost her academic scholarship and could not return to the university. I was extremely disappointed because we planned to be roommates for the spring semester. Next, I was placed on academic probation. All the partying and drinking interfered with my already struggling academic performance (imagine that). The financial aid office put me on notice that I had one more semester to improve my grades or I could not return to college. Would you believe I was on academic probation at the same time I was on judicial probation?

I had a problem with following the rules and obeying the law. So, I broke the law, and the consequence was 24-months of court-ordered probation for a petty misdemeanor crime. Therefore, both of these probations jolted me into a quick reality. I needed to change my decisions and behavior, or I would have a long, hard road ahead. But this reality wasn't an easy or quick shift in my mindset or behavior pattern because I still put myself in dangerous and thoughtless situations.

Like the time that I partied hard, drinking a 40oz and smoking weed, and went to a grocery store because I had the munchies: I walked in high, hungry and broke, but walked out high, hungry and with a stack of rib-eye steaks under my jacket. It was a foolish act that could have resulted in severe consequences. Or the time I hooked up with a guy from a different university in another state, and when he came to pick me up for the weekend, he had another guy (who I had never met) with him — and I got in the car with both guys and went across the state line for an entire weekend without telling anyone. Gratefully, I was returned safely to the campus, but it was still a stupid decision to go away with two strangers in the first place. I knew better . . . yet did not act better. I was on my way to hell in a handbasket. I did not know my purpose or my value. I was inconsiderate and inconsistent. Something had to change.

Eventually, I declared a major and set my sights to earn a two-year degree in Information Systems Technology. Therefore, I slowly began the work to shift my mindset from partying every night to only partying on the weekends and eventually not partying at all. I started to spend more time at the campus library and not the fraternity house or off-campus party. Next, I requested a private room in the dorm, so a party-girl-type roommate wouldn't tempt me to stay out all night drinking and smoking. It was a long, complicated, and often lonely road.

Most 19-year-olds are impulsive in their decision-making. Their worldview is shaped by limited experiences and lack of exposure to different people, places, or things. I was no different during my journey. I only saw the world through the narrow view of my limited experiences in Kentucky. And my only plan at the time was to get as far away from Kentucky as I could, and I did. But once I returned to Kentucky, after my time in Texas, Allison helped me put things in perspective. Although we were very close and did a lot of things together, Allison's mindset was on a completely different level than mine. Her wisdom was instrumental in guiding me to shift my mindset from "I can't" to "Maybe I can."

Sadly, in August 1993, my good friend Allison died unexpectedly. She was 23 years old and had just completed her bachelor's degree earlier that same year, only weeks away from starting her graduate program at Western Kentucky University.

A loved one's death is never an easy reality to accept, especially when that loved one is the same age as you and is your best friend. The news shook our rural community. I found out right before my fall semester was to start.

That day I walked into the house on Clay Street and was hit with more than the sweltering heat and humidity that August in Kentucky brought to its residence. When I got closer to Mama Pauline, who sat at the dining room table, I saw a strange look on her face. It was a cross between shock and grief. I never saw her look like that before. She asked when was the last time I had talked with Allison. I could not pin down the date that we had last spoke. Although we attended the same university, once we were in the flow of our course load, we didn't see each other that much. Remember, Allison was much more serious about her learning than I was; she had academic goals to achieve and did not let anything or anyone get in her way. Not to mention, she finally made time to explore a relationship and began to date a guy who lived near the university. So, on top of going to class and having a boyfriend, she didn't have time for much else.

We hung out quite a bit during my first year on campus; however, by the time I had become a sophomore, she was a junior focused on completing her undergraduate degree and moving directly into her graduate program. For summer breaks, I returned home, and she stayed on campus to complete an internship. We were still friends; however, we moved in different directions with different goals. It had been a while since we talked with each other. Once I briefly explained this to Mama, she asked me to call Allison's mother because she heard something terrible happened. I turned on my heels, went into the girl's bedroom, and picked up the phone to dial the number.

Allison's parents still lived in the house around the corner from Clay Street — I knew the number by heart and dialed it as my mind raced with what news I would find on the other end. The phone rang and rang, and then the answering machine clicked to begin the greeting. The voice who greeted the caller and gave instructions to leave a message was Allison's. I was just about to leave a message when the recorder clicked off, and the faint voice of her older sister spoke up. I said, "Hello," and her sister recognized my voice and began to cry.

Through her tears, she confirmed the news that Mama already knew but did not want to believe. "Allison passed away this morning. Allison is dead."

I dropped the phone and ran to Mama's arms, where I fell into a wave of unbearable grief and shock. Approximately a year and a half later, Allison's father died in a car accident.

CHAPTER 4

Good Grief

"Dearest friends, when I was there with you, you were always so careful to follow my instructions. And now that I am away you must be even more careful to do the good things that result from being saved, obeying God with deep reverence shrinking back from all that might displease him." *- Philippians 2:12*

ALLISON'S DEATH STIRRED UP something in me that I could not quite explain. She was a young, vibrant girl, from a wonderful family, with a good head on her shoulders. How could she be gone at such a young age? I did not know how to cope with losing a friend, so I turned to the things that had been my outlet for coping: sex, drugs, and alcohol. I threw myself into whatever bottle was open and under whatever guy who gave me attention. If the blunt was rolled, I smoked it. If there were no papers to roll the blunt, then I happily wrapped my lips on a bong.

I valued nothing about myself, and although I was nearing the end of my college experience at Western Kentucky University, I had no idea what to do next. All I knew was that in May 1994, I would return to the small, green house with the aluminum siding on Clay Street with my Associate's Degree and no job prospects, little opportunity in the surrounding community to do anything different even with a college education and student loan debt. I was a bit older than my careless high school days, but not any wiser. My mindset was fixed, so I decided to settle into working whatever job I was offered and live in my small rural community.

I owned a 1990 Honda Prelude, and although I wrecked it twice (once my fault, drunk driving; the other, not my fault, rear-ended and had it repaired twice), I had somewhat dependable transportation and took the first job offered to me, which was a 20-minute commute, one way. It was administrative work for an insurance agency. I was on the job for maybe two weeks when Daddy Boots took sick and was admitted to the hospital.

Daddy came from a generation of men who did not go to the doctor unless it was absolutely necessary. He also grew up with a cigarette in his hand and smoked for most of his life. Although everybody noticed that Daddy's health had been failing for quite some time — the evidence was in the bloody napkin he held to his mouth when he coughed — no one could convince him to go to the doctor. He could barely walk from the couch to the bathroom without losing his breath. When the time came for everyone to make the two-hour drive to Western Kentucky University to attend my college graduation, Daddy could not go. He wasn't up for all the walking.

Somewhere toward the end of July 1994, Daddy Boots finally agreed to see a doctor. The results of his visit confirmed what most of us knew, even him. He had lung cancer and was scheduled for surgery just days after he was admitted to the hospital.

Surgery day came, and we all gathered around his bed to pray. After surgery, the doctors explained they removed an entire lung and half of the other due to the cancer's advancement. Mama remained strong, but I knew she was hurting.

This was a man she had been with her entire life — they had built a good life, a good family, and parented generations of children, grandchildren, and great-grandchildren together. My sister and I looked at each other, unsure what to do but knowing that it was out of our control. Daddy Boots would spend his remaining time in the intensive care unit. The next day, Mama Pauline, my younger sister, and I returned to the hospital to visit Daddy in ICU. He was hooked up to multiple machines, all beeping and breathing for him. The nurse informed us that he had not been conscious at all that day, but his vital signs were somewhat stable considering the severity of the surgery.

The three of us stood beside his bed with only the noise of the machines filling up the silence. We all held hands. At some point, Daddy opened his eyes. He slowly looked around and reached out his hand for us to take it. Next, he slightly lifted his head and looked at each of us. He did not speak, only looked at us. We all silently filled with hope at his sudden alertness. His lips curved up to make a smile, and then he closed his eyes and laid his head back down. The next morning, I had only been at work for about an hour when I got the call. The nurse told Mama that overnight, Daddy took a turn for the worse, and we all needed to get to the hospital. Late July 1994, Daddy passed away — he was 81 years old. He had prided himself on being the provider and protector of his family. He was a hard worker and a supportive husband. He was my great-grandfather, but he was the only father I ever knew.

When a loved one passes away, grief is a unique journey. But there are some levels of grief that are so deep that only the grace of God can bring you through to arrive on the other side, look back, and say, "thank you". When Allison died, it hit me hard because it was without warning. We were the same age, shared similar experiences, and had our whole future ahead of us. Although my initial way of coping with the loss was in the form of hurting myself through sex, drugs, and alcohol, I eventually faced the sobering fact that she was not coming back, and my life had to go on. In the meantime, when Daddy Boots died, I was sad, and I missed him, but his illness had progressed over time, and on some level, I grieved the loss of him before he had physically passed away. But after his funeral, I immediately went to work, meaning that I went to work taking care of Mama Pauline.

This new role involved me as the primary person to care for her, which meant I took her to doctor appointments, ran errands, and made sure she had what she needed.

By this time, most of the relatives who once occupied the small greenhouse on Clay Street had moved out to start their own families in neighboring towns, and some even moved out of state. My younger sister and I were the last to live in the house. As she made plans to attend college and begin her future, I decided to remain at home and take care of Mama Pauline. She never learned to drive. Daddy was her chauffer, which was customary for the time that they grew up. Now that Daddy had passed away, I had no choice but to step in and take care of Mama like she had taken such good care of me all those years. It also meant that I had to take care of my great-uncle because Mama was the primary caregiver for one of her older brothers.

Born in 1916, Mama was a daughter of sharecroppers. She had three sisters and nine older brothers. The age difference did not matter because Mama Pauline was a natural caregiver, and she took care of one of her older brothers most of her life.

Her brother, Steve, suffered an eye injury when he was a young boy chopping wood on the farm. Having never received the proper treatment at the time of the injury, he lost vision in one of them. Although the eye was severely damaged, it was never covered, and as a child, I noticed this older man, who was tall, slender, and handsome, had one eye that was discolored. He gained the nickname "Cat" because his eye resembled the multi-colors of a tiger-eye marble. Uncle Cat smoked a pipe, so there was the constant smell of tobacco smoke when he came around. He eventually walked with a cane that doubled as a support for his ability to walk and a guide for his inability to see. He had a gentle spirit about him, and he and Mama often sat on the front porch and talked for hours about all sorts of stuff. They were siblings and friends.

My great-uncle Cat lived around the block from Clay Street in a shotgun-style house, so he could easily get to his sister's house by simply walking around the block. He never learned to drive either due to his impaired vision, so this meant that when I ran an errand for Mama, I ran an errand for him, too. I was an Uber driver before Uber was ever a thought.

Not long after Daddy passed away, I resigned from the new job I started because Mama needed me full-time. Eventually, I worked as a teacher assistant in a local elementary school. The school was ten minutes from the house, so I was home every day by 3 p.m. I liked being in the classroom with students, so I figured I would make my assistant position work for me and started taking classes at the local community college to earn a certificate in Early Child-hood Education.

I went to class one night a week, but I loved my new responsi-bility of taking care of Mama Pauline and Uncle Cat.

CHAPTER 5

Good Lesson

"It is God's way of making us well prepared at every point, fully equipped to do good to everyone." -2 Timothy 3:17

A S MAMA PAULINE BEGAN to age, she became even wiser than she already was. After living through the deaths of numerous family members, she decided she wanted to do things differently. One day, Mama asked me to take her to see her lawyer. After much discussion, she appointed me as the power of attorney and executrix to her estate, wanting me to make decisions on her behalf in case something happened to her. Little did I know of all the lessons that would come from this one choice.

Prayer has always been part of my life. Mama Pauline and Daddy Boots made sure a firm foundation of faith was placed on the family by teaching principles of the Ten Commandments, the books of the Holy Bible, and the practice of daily prayer. Understand, Daddy was a senior member of the Deacon Board at Clay Street Baptist Church, and he often led the prayer services on Sunday mornings.

As a child, I watched in amazement at how the words that came from his mouth would bring people to tears. The deep soulful sounds of his voice filled the church as he praised God and prayed for the church, the community, and his family. Additionally, Daddy led the prayer at home before every meal as we sat around the table.

On the other hand, Mama seemed to always have a conversation with God throughout the course of any day. She believed in the miracle-working power of God through prayer. Mama often prayed about everything . . . and for everybody. Her voice sounded low, almost to a whisper. Usually, I listened and inquired who she was talking to, and she always responded, "Just having a lil' talk with Jesus." It would take several years before I realized I needed my own prayer line to God.

But, before this realization, I lived a wild and reckless life — in and out of meaningless relationships, drinking, smoking, and getting away with everything I thought I could get away with. I dated multiple men at the same time. I even dated a married man. I had no clear direction for my future. I fell into a pattern of co-dependency, abuse, and neglect with no clear idea of how to do anything different. This pattern of behavior showed up in all of my relationships. Nevertheless, in the summer of 1994, I met a man who appeared to be different than any previous guys I met before.

When we met, the attraction was immediate, even if I thought he was much shorter than the guys I tended to be most attracted to. But after a few drinks and dancing, we quickly found out we knew a lot of people in common. We shared similarities, and being the life of any party was one of them. We exchanged phone numbers and started having regular communication immediately, and he wowed me with flights to join him for long weekends wherever he was, showering me with extravagant gifts, just because. I was awestruck. He was older than me, had built a career in the military, and had traveled the world. Although he was also from Kentucky and our families knew each other, we had never met before. And even though he would soon leave town to report to his new overseas duty station, we attached ourselves to each other during his time in the States.

So, we dated, and our relationship grew deep despite the long-distance. Meanwhile, meeting him opened my mind to a whole new world of possibilities. Although he appeared different than previous relationships, early on, I recognized patterns in his behavior that I had experienced before, but I chose to ignore the truth. In my mind, nothing could be worse than what I already experienced, so I jumped into a relationship with him with both feet. I knew if this relationship became more serious, it meant I would leave Kentucky again.

It would be around this time that I started actively keeping a journal. When it came to processing my emotions, I always internalized everything. What I mean is: if I expressed how I truly felt about a situation or what was really on my mind and was met with opposition or made to feel too sensitive or even crazy, then I would become withdrawn and quiet. That's because I did not know how to process my feelings positively or communicate them effectively. I was insecure and did not value my own ideas, thoughts, or feelings. My emotional well-being was in a constant state of flux.

Growing up in a household with multiple people but no biological parent, I felt unheard and not seen. These feelings only intensified as I got older, which is why I put so much energy into seeking acceptance through co-dependent behavior. From the beginning, I simply wanted to be heard and seen. Outside of the consistent safety and security that Mama Pauline gave me, I never found that type of support anywhere else. I recognized the destructive pattern in my behavior and attitude but did not know how to do anything different. Meanwhile, I kept a journal of my thoughts in an effort to simply get the noise out of my head in my search for clarity. So, on September 16, 1995, I purchased a new journal for $1 and started writing about the confusion I had over yet another toxic relationship.

> **09/16/1995**
>
> I am feeling some pain. But not only pain, also confusion over something I discovered two nights ago. I have been trying to do everything to get my mind off of it, but it doesn't work. I have so many questions because all the pieces of this puzzle don't fit.

Well, it was no secret that another toxic relationship would send me reeling, but this relationship was different, or at least I thought. But when I discovered something that contradicted what he told me, my mind spun out of control.

It would take close to two years of me pouring my soul out into my journal about his manipulative behavior before I could recognize a pattern in my writing and decide to slowly shift to having a more positive attitude about things and putting more positive thoughts on paper.

So, I wrote…

> **03/09/1998**
>
> This is an attempt to put some positivity into my life… I am at a point in my life where I can either get down in the dumps and wallow

in my own self-pity, or I can turn everything around and rejoice in knowing everything is going to be alright. I'm also making an attempt to put some discipline in my life. To become more grounded spiritually, emotionally and physically. I will pray more and drink more water! I know it will not be easy, change is not, but I hope to make improvements for my wellbeing. I must develop a strong sense of character. I must develop a philosophy in my life.

Overcoming

CHAPTER 6

Good Living

> "Everyone enjoys giving good advice and how wonderful it is to
> be able to say the right thing at the right time." - *Proverbs 15:23*

S
O, IT WAS IN the summer of 1994 when I met Mr. Military, and
although we were on-again, off-again for four years, we decided
to get married at the end of 1998. By this time, he was stationed
in Hawaii. At first, I was reluctant to leave Kentucky because I was
unsure of who would take care of Mama Pauline. Because although
she had aged, she was still in somewhat good health regardless of
her history with hypertension and diabetes, which were managed
with medication and regular doctor visits. And even though there
were plenty of family members nearby to watch over her, they all
had full-time responsibilities with their own families and careers.

When I knew that I would make a decision that moved me away,
I went straight to Mama Pauline and sought her wisdom first. I sat
at her feet and told her my hopes and dreams; she knew I always
wanted to go beyond our small town's boundaries and the limited

options Kentucky had to offer. I also shared my fears with her, and she looked me in my eyes and told me, "I have lived my life. I have done all that I am going to do. This is your opportunity to see the world. You go, and you do. Don't you be afraid, for God is with you wherever you go, and He is with me, too. It will be alright." What she said to me was the excellent advice I needed to move forward. We both cried at the realization that I would soon pack my bags and leave Clay Street again for a new journey to start my new life. But, relocating to Hawaii was an even greater transition than when I moved to Texas.

My future husband was already stationed in Hawaii, so I embraced this opportunity and decided to have my wedding in Hawaii. None of my family members attended the wedding, and my gown was ruined on the flight over. You would think those two incidents would cause me to pause and rethink some things, but it did not stop me — I was on a mission.

And in December 1998, at the age of 27, I got married.

Meanwhile, my move to Hawaii gradually shifted my perspective about a lot of things. Hawaii opened my world and forced me to grow and grow some more. Hawaii was a tropical paradise filled with breathtaking views and fantastic warm weather. But to live and work on the island of Oahu was difficult. And this difficulty showed me a different side of the island and set me on the path to becoming culturally self-aware and self-assured about a lot of things.

By this time, I had formed a habit of writing in my journal — mostly at night before I went to sleep or first thing in the morning when I woke up. I kept a notebook beside my bed. This allowed me to give voice to the innermost thoughts that were in my head. I would write for a few minutes with the intent of filling up a page. I always included the current date and time and would just let the pen flow on the paper. Then, after a few minutes of freewriting, I put the pen down, closed the notebook, and moved on.

04/26/1999

I woke up this morning feeling BLAH! To be honest, it seems like I've experienced this blah feeling ever since I got here, except for my wedding day. But that day had its own drama leading up to it. But since then the blah-ness keeps coming back. And I can't say it will go away when I get a job and start working...

05/21/1999

I woke up this morning with a song by Shirley Caesar playing in my head. And I have come too far to turn around... Sometimes, God as a way of taking you out of your comfort zone, placing you in a place or situation, where you don't really know how or why but you do know you've got to press on just a little more. HE also has a way of turning you around where all of your focus is on HIM. And what I just described paints the picture of my last five months here in beautiful Hawaii. Transition is hard to do.

I don't care what anybody says, change is a hard pill to swallow. But I'm easing my way and swallowing this hard pill real slow and with plenty of water. Maybe that's why God had me spend this time so far away from home, in a place that is surrounded by water, so I would have plenty of water to help me get this pill down my throat. But each day is a learning experience and that's the true blessing in all of this.

Life is to be lived, loved and learned. And I thank God for this opportunity HE has given me to learn more and more about life.

Hawaii taught me a lot about myself. I was alone most of the time because my husband had a grueling military training schedule that led up to a seven-month deployment to Japan. In his absence, I navigated the tropical paradise on my own but spent most of my time within the comfort of the military base. We were assigned a house on the base, and even though I was within walking distance to a beach, I rarely went outside.

Eventually, I found a job through a temp agency and worked for a few weeks at a local private school as a teacher assistant. I was surrounded by people with naturally darker skin than mine but was still considered an outsider because I was from the mainland, connected to the military, and Black. One time I tried to lead a circle time activity with a group of elementary students and could not make it through the lesson without a boy who raised his hand and asked, "Why are your lips pink and purple?" The lead teacher later explained that it was the first time most of the students had ever seen a Black person up close.

Nevertheless, I made friends with other military families. I even had a friend I met as a student at Western Kentucky University on the island with her new husband, who was also in the military. We saw each other occasionally. I joined a book club and even became a Key Volunteer for other military families, but it was no substitute for the homesickness I suffered.

My first Thanksgiving as a military wife, I was alone in my base housing unit and called the little green house on Clay Street to wish Mama Pauline a Happy Thanksgiving. She answered the phone with a vibrant and jubilant voice. Everything in the energy of her voice told me she was happy. She was surrounded by lots of family with plenty of food. I was the only family member not there. Mama passed the phone around to let everyone say hello to me. I heard loud laughter in the background with bits and pieces of stories being told. Keep in mind that this was back when long distances phone calls were super expensive, so I didn't stay on the phone long, but long enough for my homesickness to intensify. I hung up the phone and cried like a baby.

Living in Hawaii was challenging. Each time I drove across the island, on Highway 1, I looked at the majestic mountains that reached from the ground to the sky and said this simple prayer, "Lord, give me the strength to climb the mountain." I was not confident enough to explore the island on my own or take advantage of all the rich cultural history; instead, I relied heavily on the comfort zone and familiarity the military base offered and spent a lot of time at the base public library reading a lot of books. Over time, I became brave and decided to travel from Hawaii to Japan on a solo trip to visit my husband for our first anniversary. And this travel experience helped to shift my mindset and adopt a more global perspective.

Here's what happened: The flight to Japan was supposed to be seamless, or so I thought. I flew on a Military Aircraft Carrier or MAC flight, which cost me nothing in monetary value; however, time, flexibility, and patience are critical traits to possess. Generally, a MAC flight has one objective, complete a military mission, but if the aircraft has room for passengers and the stars all align, a passenger can get a seat on the plane and fly for free. Keep in mind that the passenger is NOT the priority; the military mission is the priority.

So, here I was, flying from Hawaii to Japan on a MAC flight all by myself, a far cry from the Trailway bus ride from Texas to Kentucky. The MAC flight stopped in Guam, per the mission, but once the plane landed, it needed maintenance (imagine that); thus, I spent my first night in Guam in the passenger air terminal.

By this time, writing in my journal was second nature, and I hardly ever left home without my notebook, so that I could capture whatever I was feeling whenever the mood hit. Therefore, as I tried to settle in for a night at Andersen Air Force Base, Guam, I got my pen and notebook out of my bag and started to write.

> **12/15/1999**
> Well, I've made it to Guam and now I sit in a passenger terminal until the plane and crew are ready to go. So, I'm trying to make the best out of two plastic chairs with a hard wooden table in the middle. This will be my bed.

That night in Guam turned into two, and after the second night, my husband purchased a ticket for me to take a commercial flight from Guam to Okinawa with a stop in Narita, Japan. And it was in Narita that I became more culturally self-aware than I ever had in my life. I went from flying from one military base to the next, where I was surrounded by Americans who spoke English, to a civilian flight in a foreign country, and I was the only person who spoke English.

After the flight touched down in Narita, Japan, two things were immediately apparent to me. Number one, I was the tallest person in the airport. I stood five feet, six inches, and was surrounded by people who were mostly four feet tall. As I walked through the airport, I was the tallest and the darkest person in the whole place. The second thing I noticed was that the energy of the Narita airport moved at rapid super-speed. There seemed to be no flight delays, only a flurry of activity with people moving fast and flights taking off on time!

I stood in the airport, looked at my boarding pass, and then looked around to find the only word I recognized in Japanese, "Okinawa." I matched symbols on my boarding pass to the symbols in the gate area where I stood but did not find a gate with the word "Okinawa" for the next departing flight. I became anxious, nervous, scared, and instinctively I looked around for a phone booth to call my husband and let him know I made it to Narita and hopefully would be on my way to Okinawa.

I found a phone but immediately noticed that it required money to use. I had a few dollar bills on me but needed coins to use the phone. Without much thought, I took my American one-dollar bill to the cashier at a kiosk and asked for some change to use the phone. She looked at me and smiled. I looked at her and smiled. She spoke Japanese. I spoke English. Our smiles represented the only language we could use to communicate with one another. I showed her my dollar bill with George Washington displayed on the front, and she smiled and simply shook her head back and forth, which told me, "No."

This was 1999. No cell phones. No wireless Internet. No Google Translate. I felt a rush of fear at the reality that I was in Japan without a lifeline to let anyone know where I was. I then noticed a symbol that resembled a bathroom and went in to collect my thoughts and use the toilet. I walked in and saw a stall with a hole directly in the floor. But there was a stall at the end of the row with the word "Western" on the door. I opened that door and saw the familiar sight of a porcelain toilet, upright and above ground. I opted for the Eastern way and used the toilet directly in the floor. As I washed my hands, I looked at myself in the mirror and laughed;

it was all I could do to keep from crying. Next, I prayed and asked God to give me the strength to make it to my destination.

After I walked out of the restroom, I refocused on finding the departure gate with the flight headed to Okinawa. Again, I matched symbols, and everything checked out to let me know I was in the right place — all but the word "Okinawa." I showed my boarding pass to the ticket agent, and she pointed me to two gates down. No words were spoken; the language barrier was universal, but so was the smile on the face, the point of the hand, or the nod of the head.

I walked two gates down, showed my ticket to a different ticket agent, who only pointed me back in the direction I had just left. By this time, any calmness that I had was quickly developing into a full-blown panic attack because flights were being announced on the intercom, and planes were leaving the runway for take-off with precision. I could not risk being stranded in an airport again.

I quick-stepped back to the first ticket agent I had communicated with just a few minutes earlier and showed her my boarding pass for the second time. With eagerness, I pointed to the word "Okinawa" on my ticket and then pointed to the overhead display board, which had a different destination. I must have looked like a Black Vanna White waving my hands and pointing at letters, but this was not a game show . . . this was serious! The ticket agent must have felt the urgency and panic in my energy (plus it was all over my face) because she eventually came from around the ticket counter to where I stood and looked up to where I pointed. Next, she went behind the counter, slammed her fist on the button that controlled the display board, and the word "OKINAWA" presented itself in bold letters. The entire display board lit up, and it felt like I had just won the bonus round. I was at the right departure gate all along, but the display board had gotten stuck and never showed the updated destination.

A smile broke out over everybody's face at this realization. By this time, I had drawn the attention of a small audience, so I clutched my chest because I had "won" a trip to Okinawa and was on my way. I then turned and waved goodbye to my adoring Japanese fans and boarded my plane, already filled with passengers.

Once in my seat, I laid my head back, closed my eyes, and whispered a word of prayer as the plane pulled away from the gate and taxied down the runway. Finally, I was on my way.

I made it safely to Okinawa, Japan. I met a lot of wonderful people, enjoyed scrumptious food, and had a great time. I even partied with my new husband and new friends like it was 1999 and brought in two-thousand-zero-zero singing karaoke. But after a month of enjoying this cultural experience, I returned to Hawaii via MAC flight and spent five nights in a passenger terminal in Yakota Air Force Base on my way back to Hickam AFB. But none of that mattered because the entire experience gave me strength and courage to overcome plenty of obstacles and cultivate a global mindset by traveling alone to an international country in Y2K.

Nevertheless, my time in Hawaii did not last forever, and soon it was time to move again. This time the next duty station was located in Washington D.C., and this move took my thinking to a whole other level.

But remember, Mama Pauline had appointed me the executrix to her estate and given me power of attorney well before my moving to Hawaii. Yet, it became difficult for me to make decisions on her behalf, if needed, when I lived so far away. So, before I relocated to Hawaii, Mama and I agreed that another family member would be issued power of attorney in my absence. This arrangement worked well while I was in Hawaii, and even after I moved to D.C.; however, now that I was back on the mainland and could keep a closer eye on Mama Pauline, I began to sense that something was wrong. Still, I kept my suspicions to myself and was just glad to be a short commercial flight from Mama.

A few months after the relocation, Mama's health began to decline. What started as a small sore on her foot became a severely infected foot ulcer and resulted in partial leg amputation due to her medical history of diabetes. At one of my many visits to her hospital bed before several surgeries leading up to the amputation, it was a rare occasion where it was just the two of us in her hospital room. She looked tired and weak, but she was strong enough to give me strict instructions on what to do and how to handle things if she could not. I sat next to her bed and held her hand. It was soft, warm, and calming, just like it always was when I held her hand. We sat in comfortable silence for a while, her eyes closed. I watched her chest move up and down. I started to get sad. Then in her quick, compassionate, humorous way, she looked at me and said, "I'm not dead yet."

Next, she told me very directly, "Pray that I'm strong enough to make it through this; but if I don't ask God to give you the strength to go on." I cried. She cried. Next, she instructed me to be strong and to live my life to the fullest because I was an adult now. I told her it wasn't fun being an adult. She laughed. "I love you, Mama. I love you so much!" I said to her. "I love you, too. It's alright. It will all be alright." She replied.

To see Mama Pauline go through so much pain and anguish was a hard reality for all the family to face. Yet, we each coped with her illness as best as we knew how — mostly in the form of denial. This dysfunctional behavior pattern showed me the true character of some family members that I could no longer deny. As Mama's quality of life began to decline, those family members I was once very close to started to rise up against me in ways I could have never imagined. I slowly realized that if something happened to Mama Pauline, I would be the one who would make decisions on her behalf, and most family members did not like this arrangement. Some felt entitled and even challenged my ability to make the best decisions based on my past mistakes.

Some even decided to take advantage of the situation and lived in the small, green house with aluminum siding on Clay Street without paying any bills; the property tax, gas, electric, and Bell South all had outstanding balances. Soon, I asserted myself and gave an ultimatum to those who lived in the house to either take responsibility and contribute or find somewhere else to live. After this, I was bullied by my own family. I was hurt and disappointed by those I trusted the most.

We all dealt with Mama's approaching surgery to amputate her leg differently. Some coped with familiar vices through drinking and smoking— meanwhile, others got through this time by working a lot or not coming around. I coped with a combination of everything, but I never stopped writing in my journal. And it was around this time that I had one dream that was so life-like that I scribbled out the details not being fully awake.

Dream 4/11/01

He was half the size of a normal man. He was a dwarf. People were getting captured all around me. Then I got captured. He was amputating the hands and feet of everyone. Sometimes, just one limb, then both. You had to grab inside a box and pull out one of

> the amputated limbs; that's how it got determined which limb you
> would lose. I woke up with a pounding headache.

This was the first time I ever experienced loving someone so much
that I physically and emotionally felt their pain. I managed to put
on a brave face in public, but inside I was dying, often crying myself
to sleep at night and waking in tears. But I began to read the Bible
more and drink alcohol less in an effort to be strong like Mama
Pauline asked me to be. But I felt utterly alone, no matter where
I was or who was around me, with no one relating to what I felt.
I sensed a complete emotional breakdown, so I turned to the one
thing I knew, prayer.

In early spring 2001, Mama Pauline had her partial leg amputation surgery and recovered after several weeks in the hospital. At
one of my visits to the hospital, Mama was completely alert, and
she informed me of some suspicions she had before her surgery.

Mama Pauline received a monthly Social Security check for
$828.00 and kept a very tight budget before being hospitalized;
no bill was ever overdue. When she began to overhear talk about
outstanding balances on accounts and even the quality of her reha-
bilitation care due to insufficient funds, she suspected something
was very, very wrong — suspecting that the family member who
was her current power of attorney had made bad decisions with
her money. Naturally, she assumed that those who now took up
residence in the family home in her absence would have the decency
to keep the bills paid since everybody was able to work. So not long
after this red flag, Mama requested that I be reinstated as her power
of attorney and sole executrix to her estate. I obeyed her request
and called her attorney, a social service clinician from Cabinet for

Families and Children, and a notary to meet us in Mama's hospital room to update all of her estate planning documents.

This decision once again put certain family members against me. I ignored the hurtful comments and threats because I knew I had an obligation to Mama Pauline. I had to be brave. I had to be strong for her, no matter what.

Late summer 2001, Mama Pauline was moved to a nursing home where she could receive the round-the-clock medical attention she needed, including weekly dialysis treatment. With this arrangement, Mama Pauline was now living in the same nursing home where her brother "Cat," my great-uncle, also lived. Hence, with Mama's doubts about her finances being mishandled, I hired a social services attorney to investigate Mama's bank account activity further.

The investigation revealed that the family member not only stole money from Mama's account but also from Uncle Cat's since Mama Pauline was power of attorney over her brother. Photocopies of all bank account activity revealed checks written out for cash, groceries, and Safe Auto Insurance (Mama never drove or owned a car). When Mama selected the family member to become POA in my absence, this person had automatic access to Uncle Cat's bank accounts, who was also on a fixed income. See, Uncle Cat passed away in August 2001, and his death was not reported immediately; therefore, Social Security continued to send the monthly check, and the family member immediately took it out by writing a personal check for cash.

About a year after this incident, I received a collection notice from the bank for $503.51 because the Social Security Administration had sent a reclamation request for funds dispersed due to the owner being deceased. Still, the POA at the time did not pay the negative balance.

The facts from the investigation made me sick, literally. For the life of me, I could not figure out why anybody, especially a family member, would take advantage of Mama Pauline (or Uncle Cat). But with all the data in hand, I went to the hospital to break the news to Mama. I walked in, and although I did not give her any details from the investigation, she knew that what she had suspected was confirmed when she saw the look on my face. But we both realized that things were much worse than either of us first thought.

Mama Pauline was hurt and extremely disappointed that someone she trusted would take advantage of her and her brother. But I was pissed and wanted to press charges. Mama did not want to get the police involved more than they already were. Instead, she told me that the only thing we should do was pray. Pray for our family, pray for our friends and pray for our enemies. And that's what we did. Mama's faith in God was unshakable. She trusted that everything wrong would be made right by God's grace.

It was by her faith and forgiving spirit that she healed well enough from her partial leg amputation to spend Thanksgiving 2001 at the small green house on Clay Street, surrounded by all of her family. Yes . . . even the family member who had stolen money from her and her brother.

Mid-November 2001, I made the solo trip from D.C. to Kentucky for the early holiday gathering and prayed for strength and restraint not to knock somebody's head off for stealing from Mama Pauline and Uncle Cat. Therefore, I shifted my mind to focus on spending time with Mama at Clay Street and prayed for strength to fellowship with family members who resented me and who (I imagined) secretly wished I choked on my turkey and dressing. Of course, I wished the same for them.

Writing had now become a crucial part of my emotional well-being. So much swirled through my head I felt like I spun out of control, even when I sat still or slept. I made sure to write during my trip home to Kentucky, but I only wrote on the plane ride to and from because I wanted to be fully present during my visit with Mama. I captured this entry on my way back to Baltimore Washington International Airport. I had a window seat, where I could look out and connect with the clouds and let my feelings flow.

> **11/18/2001**
>
> *When I think of home, I think of a place where there is love overflowing... Nothing is more important than family! If this trip taught me anything, making the effort to get home to be with Mama was well worth the trip. Mama's face was in a constant beam as she sat in the comfort of her own home and watched all of her children gather for an early Thanksgiving. It was truly beautiful. I am truly blessed! Thank you, Jesus, for this day. Thank you for my safe journey and protection. More importantly, thank you for my Family!*

I traveled between D.C. and Kentucky quite a bit, as there was a direct flight within my budget. We had only been in the Washington area since May of 2001, and I had begun working for the federal government by mid-June. I adjusted to this move a bit more than I did when I moved to Hawaii, navigating D.C.'s metro system and diving into the "go-go" rhythm of my new city . . . and then the September 11 terrorist attacks happened.

My professional life quickly became really interesting due to the nature of my work in the office of security and counterintelligence.

My stress level was through the roof, and my emotional well-being was in constant flux. Every area of my life, personally and professionally, had its own drama. The majority of the time, I woke up uncertain of anything, not even my name.

By the beginning of 2002, Mama's health was on a quick decline with multiple dialysis treatments every week. I traveled extensively at this time due to my job. I was mentally and physically exhausted, but I took every opportunity to fly home to Kentucky because I knew that Mama Pauline needed me. I needed her. Early in March, during one of my visits, Mama was rushed to the hospital due to fluid on her lungs. She became stable enough to return to the nursing home, but this became the pattern over the next few weeks.

March 7, 2002, I made a trip to Kentucky and did not tell anyone of my travel plans. I got off the plane and went straight to the nursing home. I walked into Mama's room, and she was coherent enough to recognize me. Her face lit up, and she smiled when she saw me. No words, just a smile, then she drifted back to sleep. I stayed by her bedside for as long as the nursing home allowed visitation. The next day, I boarded a plane and returned to Washington. Sadly, on April 13, 2002, Mama died of heart failure. She was 86.

I had felt sick to my stomach that entire day and never could explain why. Meanwhile, I shuffled through the day of errands and whatnot. It was a Saturday, and after putting it off multiple times, I had finally agreed to accept a dinner invite to a co-worker's house who lived in Virginia while my husband and I lived in Maryland. We made the drive and planned to spend the evening getting to know my co-worker and his wife and enjoying his extensive collection of Earth, Wind, and Fire live concert videos.

Not long after we finished an authentic Puerto Rican dinner and retreated to their newly built media room, the cell phone rang. Cookie's voice shouted loud, asking me where I'd been because the hospital and nursing home had been calling my home phone all day. Before I could even explain, she shouted, "It's Mama! Mama done died!" My world completely fell apart. I was devastated; grief and depression stood at the threshold of every room I entered. All I wanted to do was crawl in a hole and not come out, but I couldn't — everybody was waited on me to get home to make final arrangements.

I left for Kentucky the next morning. I had to be strong. I had to be brave. I had work to do.

CHAPTER 7

Good Faith

"The good man's life is full of light. The sinner's road is dark and gloomy." -Proverbs 13:9

I WAS BROUGHT UP TO have a strong belief in God. I was also taught the values of self-awareness, self-acceptance, and self-determination. Even when I knew all these things and still chose to do the wrong thing, the power of prayer and faith provided the most meaning to my life. The journey was not easy, yet I believed. I arrived in Kentucky and prepared myself for whatever was ahead as it related to making funeral arrangements for Mama Pauline.

I was staying at a friend's house during this time, and one night, I had fits of sleep. I woke one morning and reached for my notebook to intentionally capture my feelings. It was the worst pain I had ever felt, and I realized that whatever I was experiencing, I had to acknowledge it because it would be vital to me moving forward.

So, I wrote:

April showers rained down, and Mama's funeral played out worse than I could have imagined. The tension throughout the family was undeniable. None of us knew how to behave towards each other in a respectful and compassionate way now that Mama Pauline was gone. Although she had prearranged her funeral, insurance covered the maximum amount, but there was still an outstanding balance. And just because the house on Clay Street had no mortgage payment, taxes and utility bills had mounted up. The general assumption from most family members was that since I was in charge, I should pay for everything. Plus, it was also assumed that since I married a military man and we lived and worked in D.C., we had the money to take care of everything. All of these assumptions were false in every way.

Friday night was the visitation, and after it was over, I tried to solicit family to help with some of the funeral's outstanding expenses. I had been given the silent treatment by most of the family, which was not uncommon. The pattern was to deal with serious issues by not talking about them. Meanwhile, those who still communicated with me had only done so for their personal benefit with no real genuine interest in how I felt but what I could do for them.

So, after friends and extended family had left the church, I stood in front of all the immediate family, all of those who I had grown up with at that little house. Some sat and glared at me; others had side conversations as if my standing there did not matter. And I guess to most of them... it didn't.

I inhaled. I exhaled, and then I asked for financial donations to cover the remaining balance of $769. I received a total of $475, which included a hundred from my husband and me, with the rest coming from four grandchildren, a missionary organization Mama participated in, and a neighboring friend who lived on Clay Street. Meanwhile, others responded with mumbled, "I ain't got no money for this." "She got all the money!" "This is a damn shame." Not long after, most of them got up and walked out of the church. I stood strong in front of everyone, but after the church was empty, I wrapped myself around Mama's casket and cried my heart out. At that moment, I wanted to get in the coffin with her.

The funeral was the next day, and things got even worse. Clouds covered the sky, and the rain sprinkled. I had a massive headache and wanted to stay hidden under the covers, but I couldn't. I had to get up. I had to honor Mama Pauline.

The immediate family met at the funeral home for the processional, while the dark and gray clouds represented the tense energy emanating from everyone. Some members gathered inside, while others bunched under the protective covering outside. There was shouting and screaming at some point, and then the next thing I knew, two family members were fighting. At this same time, Cookie and one of her brothers had their own shouting match in the funeral home parking lot. The funeral directors had to bring order to the chaos to get us all to the church on time for the funeral to start. And it was at that moment that I mentally checked out from everything and everybody. I did not want to be around my family, and any relationship that I had with any of them forever changed in that instant.

Once the graveside burial was over, I did not go back to the church for the repast. Instead, I met a few close friends for dinner at a restaurant, and I drank margaritas until I passed out, literally. I was beyond exhausted and overcome with grief, and on the plane ride to BWI, I vowed to never return to Kentucky. I was done with my family. And, once back in D.C., I forged through the demands of my job, plus I had enrolled in yet another community college. I welcomed every distraction to my grief.

Before I knew it, I was on a plane yet again headed to New Mexico for a business conference. I lived at the airport and out of my suitcase for two weeks straight after Mama Pauline passed away. However, instead of seeing my travel as a means to escape, everything irritated me, and my exhaustion was beyond anything I had ever experienced. But, time, distance, prayer, forgiveness, and faith somehow brought peace in the midst of the chaos.

My journal notebook was still laid by my bedside, but days would go by, and I would not write anything. I just wanted to sleep and wake from the daily nightmare I was in without any written record of how I felt. But one night, in New Mexico, I couldn't sleep, so I grabbed my notebook and pen and tried to sort things out.

05/01/2002
Everything is wrong. Nothing is right. Will I ever see any light at the end of this dark, long tunnel? This trip to New Mexico has been

> very irritating and exhausting. Damn! So much for thinking I would get a little rest and relaxation. It seems like everything is going on — but nothing is really happening. In the meantime, I know one thing that didn't happen in April. My period!

I returned to D.C. on a Friday evening, and first thing the following morning, I drove to Target and bought a home pregnancy test.

I went straight to the bathroom as soon as I got back home. The stick turned pink and positive before I could lay it on the counter for the required three minutes for results. I sat on the toilet, completely gripped with fear. No way could this be happening to me. No fucking way. Not now.

I went and got my husband off the couch and brought him to the bathroom. I pointed to the stick. I couldn't find the words to speak. He looked at the stick and immediately started jumping up and down with excitement. He had wanted to start a family as soon as we were married. But for five years, we had tried with no success, so this pink stick that indicated that I was pregnant sent him over the moon with enthusiasm. While he laughed and danced in the mirror, I cried.

The magic of pregnancy was very hard for me to realize and accept early on. I was grief-stricken and couldn't find any ray of light in my dark world. So, I made an appointment with the doctor to confirm what a Target pregnancy test already told me. Yes, I was indeed pregnant. The doctor placed the small monitor on my belly, and the swishing and thumping beat of the baby's heart rang crystal clear throughout the room. The heartbeat of my baby brought my broken heart back to life. It was then that I decided to appreciate the miracle of life that grew inside me and began the slow process of enjoying the journey of pregnancy.

In spite of this, initially, I was angry, especially with God, because he had taken Mama away from me when I would need her most. I thought my missed menstrual cycle was due to the extreme stress I was under. I looked back and saw how my fatigue was not just connected to my grief; it was also linked to my need for rest in order for new life to grow and spring forth. I bought the book *What to Expect When You are Expecting*, and I bought a pregnancy journal to chronicle this life-changing event. Yet, I found myself caught between joy and grief. So, it was in my second trimester, at a prenatal appointment, that a simple question, "How are you doing today?" erupted tears that would not stop. This prompted the doctor to recommend that I see a therapist.

My therapy sessions were intense, and after my first visit, I cried myself sick sitting in the car in the parking lot. I vowed never to go back to therapy and was very close to losing all hope of fully healing from the pain. But once I crawled into bed that night, I reached over and grabbed the two things that had remained constant in my life at that point, my journal and a pen.

07/23/2002

Nobody understands me. Nobody! I had my first therapy session and I left feeling like it was a disaster. I had so much to say but as usual couldn't find the right way to say it. As a result, things just got screwed up, as usual. I'm just tired of all of this shit! I truly am! Lord, I need you! Mama I need you. I wish you were here. I wish I was with you.

My balance as a grieving woman and soon-to-be mother was off. Some days I managed okay. Then there were moments I looked at a picture of Mama Pauline or heard her voice in a dream, and I would lose it. But the closer I got to my due date, the more I longed for Mama to be with me. I was scared and had no clue how to be a mother.

I received love, affection, protection, sensitivity, empathy, compassion, consistency, and acceptance from one person, and that was Mama Pauline. She was more than a mother to me, and it's still hard to find words to articulate just how much she meant to me. Meanwhile, what I received from Cookie came in the form of an envelope full of money or visits twice a year. Cookie did not have the capacity to give me all the things I needed most.

Although therapy started to get a little better with weekly sessions, it was still hard for me to sit across from someone and hear them analyze my behavioral patterns and generational dysfunction. As a result, I turned to the most constant thing I had in my life, my journal notebook and a pen.

> 11/19/2002
>
> Although Mama is always on my mind, I manage to get through each day. Then, there are moments when I look at her picture and think back and try to relive every moment. The closer I get to having my first child, the more I long for Mama to be here with me, to hold my hand and reassure me that everything would be okay. That I would be okay.

However, nothing about my pregnancy or delivery went without risk; I was a 31-year old, Black female with a family history of hypertension. Even though my blood pressure spiked from time to time during pregnancy, it never got to the point of preeclampsia. Nevertheless, my unborn baby had its own set of risks while in the womb.

First, the doctors noticed a two-vessel cord baby, which meant the baby was at risk for not being fully developed in some areas due to loss of nutrients. Secondly, my baby was breech. Even after the External Cephalic Version procedure, the baby remained in a breeched position. This confirmed that I would bring a very strong, determined, and independent-minded individual into this world. But before I could give birth to new life, I had business from an old life that I had to handle.

Family members continued to live in the small house on Clay Street after Mama passed away, and bills continued to be past due. Jealousy and envy clouded any rational judgment for anyone to step up and take accountability because everyone counted on me to take care of everything since I was the one left "in charge."

So, I did. I took charge and gave everyone the opportunity to purchase the property so that they would have the freedom to do whatever they wanted to do, and I would stop getting overdue or collection notices. Yet no one stepped up. Therefore, as the executrix of her estate, I decided to put the property up for sale. This decision was met with even more threats and bullying, and craziness. I had family members go as far as call me in the middle of the night and threatened to burn the house down or threatened to sue me for putting them out because they had nowhere else to go and they had a right to be there. But the threat that I remembered most was a family member who threatened to take the aluminum siding off the house because it had to be worth some money. Through this experience, the lesson I learned was that the death of a loved one brings out the best and the worst in people, but whatever is revealed, believe it!

Mind you, I was pregnant, and everybody knew it; however, it did not stop the bullying. Somehow, I gathered up the supernatural strength necessary for me to sell the house. This also meant I was responsible for cleaning out the residence of all of its belongings, which included the current occupants. So, the weekend that I flew to Kentucky to clean house, I assembled a small group of friends to help me pack, load, and haul furniture to Goodwill and storage. I went through every inch of the small house to clean out closets, empty dressers, and preserve pictures and other important documents.

As I did this, I came across a small tethered book, held together by some worn binding tape. The book had my name on it. It was a children's story I had written while in elementary school. I sat on the floor and read the book, and tears streamed down my face. I cried because reading that little story confirmed for me what I had known in my heart. I was a writer. And Mama kept that elementary school assignment all those years because she knew I was a writer too.

After the house was completely packed up, and all the boxes and furniture were moved out, I stood in the center and cried. All my life, the house was filled with voices, laughter, and food. What was once a vibrant place of love, family, and fellowship, now sat empty. My heart ached for the turmoil I currently found myself in with my family. But the ache was replaced with peace because I knew I did what Mama trusted me to do. I longed to have Mama with me, not only for guidance on handling family matters but also for guidance on motherhood. Around this time, Mama appeared to me in a dream.

> **8/23/2002**
> I dreamt that I had a baby girl and Mama finally met her. My daughter had just woken from a nap. I changed her diaper and put on a warm outfit and when I walked in the room, Mama's face lit up with a smile. With a laugh in her voice she told me that my daughter was the cutest little thing. The three of us walked over to the mirror to see our reflection, our generation, and our love. I said, "Look Mama, she has our nose and our mouth." Mama replied, with a smile on her face, "She sure does, she is the cutest little thing." My daughter laughed with glee and reached for Mama. Mama took her great-great grandchild in her arms and rocked her close to her bosom. My daughter quickly fell back to sleep.

I ached to have Mama with me. Meanwhile, each therapy session became more and more intense. I was in so much pain and completely broken. The next therapy session would come, and I sat on the couch and cried my heart out to a stranger who made me face trauma I didn't even know I had. My brokenness started way before Mama passed away. My hurt happened way before the turmoil with my family after Mama died. Somewhere along the way, a deep seed of jealousy and resentment was planted within the family, especially among the women, except for Mama. A seed developed over time that overflowed with selfishness, confusion, and drama among certain family members. And this happened way before I was born.

Jealousy was a vicious disease and caused a lot of pain. As a young girl, I overheard conversations about me being had by family members that were not favorable or loving — the comments filled with meanness and hatred towards me. I always felt different and struggled with where I fit in, even with a house full of people. Mama was my protector in a lot of ways. While some of the resentment was directed towards Cookie for not taking care of me, since she wasn't around much, I became the receiver of all of it. I grew up and was afraid that I would be abandoned. My insecurities set me up, so I did not know how to set boundaries, and I lacked the emotional maturity to express my authentic self. Thus, I conditioned myself to accept how people treated me, no matter how it made me feel. This turmoil built up in me, and I didn't even realize it.

Around this same time, my marriage had started to show signs of being on shaky ground. I did not want to deal with any of my junk. My denial ran deep. I had a victim mentality and became skilled at denying my truth. Therapy helped me to uncover the trauma that I had suppressed from childhood. If I wanted a different future, I had to release my past. But first, I had to get through my childhood.

Cookie was not there for me as I grew up, and although I saw her twice a year, our bond was deeply dysfunctional. But when Cookie came to visit, it was like Christmas. I stood at the door and waited for her arrival. And when she arrived, she had loads of gifts for everyone. But after the initial excitement wore off and all the gifts were opened, she withdrew to the bed where she would be in a coma-type sleep for days with her head completely covered by the blanket — sound asleep. She only got up to eat and use the bathroom. When she finally got up to engage in anything, it was to play card games with friends who had stopped by or to entertain the company of a 'special friend' when he arrived.

The special friend seemed to be someone different every time. This abandonment set me on a path to be needed and accepted by anyone, no matter the cost to my health, safety, or self-esteem. And although Mama Pauline and Daddy Boots sacrificed so much to give me a life of love, stability, and support, I grew up carrying the baggage of guilt, shame, jealousy, and resentment that was not mine to carry in the first place.

As a result, I did not value myself. Additionally, I was molested at a young age. This event's trauma was deeply suppressed for years, but it showed up as self-destruction that only intensified over time. I repressed all of this pain and truth for years. I was a complete mess, and I had a whole lot of work ahead before I gave birth to my first child. If I wanted peace and love for myself, I had to get clear. I had to own my junk, eliminate toxic thoughts, ideas, actions, beliefs, and people from my life. I had to be strong. I had to be courageous. I had so much work to do.

CHAPTER 8

Good Move

> "For God, who gives seed to the farmer to plant and later on, good crops to harvest and eat, will give you more and more seed to plant and will make it grow so that you can give away more and more fruit from your harvest." –2 Corinthians 9:10

I CONTINUED WITH INTENSE THERAPY sessions several times a week. I read inspirational books, listened to sermons and music, and continued to write in my journals. Slowly, I started to acknowledge and accept things. Very, very slowly. There were some days where all I could do was cry about all of my mess. Yet, I began to think differently about my future. Because I wasn't alone anymore, I had a baby on the way, and if I wanted my baby to have a different life, I had to make different choices.

And with that, at seven months pregnant, I interviewed and accepted a new job with a new government agency. It was a breath of fresh air to be in a different work environment. I also went to the dentist and requested some reconstructive work on my upper right quadrant.

When I was 18, I had replaced my natural tooth with an open-face gold crown, and I did not want my child influenced by my gold tooth as I had been when I saw those around me with gold teeth. So, I replaced my gold tooth with a porcelain one to match the rest of my teeth. This might not have been a big deal to most, but it was vital to me. These were seemingly minor changes, but they helped me move in the right direction to break some of the generational strongholds I uncovered about my thoughts, actions, and behaviors.

By the time I reached my third trimester, I had weekly ultra-sounds because I carried a breeched, two-vessel cord baby. And one Friday in December 2002, I stayed at the hospital the entire first shift because my fluid level dropped, and they were afraid I would go into labor at any moment. But the doctors finally decided to let me go home, with strict orders for bed rest for the remainder of the weekend and return to the hospital first thing Sunday morning. So, I left the hospital that Friday evening and went directly to the beauty shop to get my hair fixed. And on Saturday evening, I attended my company Christmas party. But early Sunday morning, I reported to the hospital per doctor's orders and was admitted. And when I was examined, it was discovered that my fluid levels were even lower than they were on Friday, plus the baby was breech, so the decision was made to prep me for a C-section.

The operating room was ice cold, and it took the anesthesiologist two attempts for the spinal tap because I was shivering so badly. But once I became numb, I lay back on the small metal table and stretched out my arms in the shape of a "T." Next, I closed my eyes and said a quick prayer. It was go-time.

Now, I had read all the books about the types of delivery, and after I knew that I had to have a C-section since the baby was breached, I knew what to expect. Or at least I thought. Nothing can ever really prepare you for childbirth, even with a scheduled C-section. Not long after I was good and numb lying on an icy metal tray table, I felt a few hard pulls and then a deep-deep tug, and with that, the doctor announced, "Congratulations, it's a girl."

My husband had a video camera in one hand and a picture camera in the other. Everything happened at rapid speed. But in the frenzy of delivery, one thing I quickly noticed was that I did not hear my baby crying. I could only hear the clicks from the camera and some muffled talk from the doctors. They quickly took my baby to the other side of the room, and a flurry of activity happened around me that I could not see. I turned my head and looked at the large clock on the wall, and I started to pray again. "Why can't I hear my baby cry?" I asked under my breath. *This is not how it happens in the movies or what I read in the books*, I thought.

I could not lift my head very high off the table to see anything. I looked around for my husband, and he was in the same area as the doctors, with the baby, snapping pictures and recording everything. I kept praying. And after what seemed like forever, I finally heard the faint cry of my newborn baby.

Later, I learned that the reason she had not cried immediately after delivery was because she had been asleep. She was tucked upside down, nestled in my womb, taking an afternoon nap. But after they had awakened her and lifted her so that I could see her, I took one look at her sweet face and broke into tears. There it was . . . she had Mama's nose. And she had my nose — the same nose that I was teased about for being too big, too wide, and too funny looking. The same nose that when I was 16, I begged Mama to let me alter so I would stop being teased. The same nose that at one time I hated now stared back at me on the beautiful face of my infant daughter. The same nose that I dreamt she would have, and she did have. It was as if I looked at a baby version of myself that somehow also looked like Mama. My heart filled with joy but also grief. I longed to have Mama Pauline beside me to see her great-great-granddaughter. Yet I knew Mama was there, in that delivery room, and I felt her spirit. I felt her peace.

My daughter was born the week before Christmas, and once we were discharged to go home, I would sit and stare at her sweet face in amazement. I could not believe that my body was selected as a vessel to bring this creative, pure positive energy being in the world. Oh, how I missed Mama Pauline's physical presence and ached for her to be beside me on this journey.

Thus, I fell into the bumpy flow of motherhood and all the real things about being a first-time mother that no one told me about, like how my stomach still looked like I was pregnant even though I held my baby in my arms; or the fact that my daughter did not immediately latch and refused to nurse from my breast. Even with several lactation specialists around my bed instructing me to squeeze my nipple like a football, my infant daughter refused and only screamed louder. I ended up pumping my breast milk and feeding her from a bottle until around three months when by chance, I put her next to my breast, and she latched onto my nipple like a pro. I sat there frozen in place, not wanting to ruin the moment or risk her falling off the nipple. Breastfeeding was a surreal experience.

And after twelve weeks of maternity leave, I enrolled my daughter in the daycare on the military base not far from my job and returned to work with a breast pump and some bottles in hand. It was so good to have the support of my new employer to balance work and motherhood. But wouldn't you know, just a few weeks after establishing a new routine and my post-pregnancy belly showing signs of going down, my husband received orders for a new duty station. It was time to relocate again, this time from Washington, D.C. to Milwaukee, Wisconsin. And it was after we moved to Wisconsin, I found myself at a crossroad.

Of course, the relocation forced me to resign from my good federal government job in Washington D.C., but I did not have the same fortune to find a job right away in Wisconsin. I was a new mom in a new city. I had to make a new decision.

Late summer 2003, as I unpacked boxes and rearranged the furniture in our rented mid-western home, I listened to the radio, which filled the quietness of our new place and new neighborhood. The suburban area of Wisconsin that we lived in was really quiet, and we were the only Black family there. My world was completely upside down. I went from Prince George's County, Maryland, to Waukesha County, Wisconsin. Meanwhile, the radio ad announced that a new location for a university would soon open. The ad continued to announce that the university's program was designed to fit the busy life of any adult who wanted to return to school, and it "accepted all previously earned credits." I stopped in my tracks because this was exactly what I needed to hear but had never heard before. I immediately wrote down the number.

Later, I called and explained my situation to the counselor and scheduled a meeting to go over my unofficial transcripts to determine if I would be a good fit for the program and possibly enroll. The day the appointment came to talk to an enrollment counselor, I had doubts. *How could I return to school now? I was a new mom in a new city. I couldn't possibly juggle going back to school after all this time.* The closer time came for me to go to my appointment with the enrollment counselor, the louder my daughter cried. I used that as an excuse and was a no-show for my appointment.

I went to bed and wished I never heard the radio ad about the new university in my area that "accepted all previously earned credits," with classes that started in a few weeks. Looking back, I wished my head wasn't filled with so much doubt.

The next day, the enrollment counselor called and rescheduled our meeting. This time I showed up with my unofficial transcripts. I was scared of the outcome but determined to move forward by a force that I could not explain. I applied and was awarded financial aid with more than enough to enroll in the accelerated eight-week term program. I became excited about school, but I still had times where I experienced grief, and motherhood was challenging in a new city with no family support close by. But being in the classroom helped me cope with everything in a more positive way and not revert to old habits of drugs or alcohol to numb my pain.

In the meantime, life hit me pretty hard between relocating from D.C. to Wisconsin. I was grief-stricken at the loss of Mama Pauline and overwhelmed with motherhood. My life went through a series of life, death, and life cycles.

My relationship with Cookie was always difficult to understand and even more of a challenge to explain. I longed to be mothered and found myself initiating phone calls to Cookie that never would've happened had I not picked up the phone. After a very shallow and forced conversation, I hung up the phone, vowing never to call her again. I felt let down and disappointed in myself for finding myself in the pattern of hoping, wishing, and praying for things to get better between us, only to feel the same empty feeling. So, to my journal notebook I went to pour out my heart.

When Mama Pauline died, Cookie tried to assert herself in my life and fill a hole that we each had, but it just didn't work. She tried to force something that just wasn't there. Mama was the seamstress that held all of us together. Now that she was gone, it was hard to navigate a simple conversation without being triggered by a past experience that only deepened any hurt or pain. The entire family suffered a great loss when Mama Pauline died, and we all struggled to find tools to truly heal, support each other, and move forward in love.

CHAPTER 9

Good Mother

> "Salvation is not a reward for the good we have done, so none of us can take credit for it." -*Ephesians 2:9*

R EMEMBER, COOKIE HAD MOVED away from Kentucky when I was a toddler, and when she would visit, we fell into a pattern that went from the honeymoon stage, to the uncertainty stage, and ultimately the divorce stage. She and I each had the capacity to have successful interpersonal relationships with friends and other family members but our mother/daughter bond struggled.

Additionally, after Mama Pauline died and I discovered I would be a mother, I decided to ALWAYS be there for my child, no matter what. I decided to break the cycle of dysfunction and create something different for my family. I moved in another direction without a clear model but with the determination to simply move forward. After I found a college program that accepted my previously earned credits, I made education and motherhood a priority, but nothing about that decision was easy.

Ottawa University designed a learning program for working adults who wanted to return to school and earn their undergraduate degrees. Classes met one night a week in the evenings from 6 p.m. – 9 p.m. On a cool mid-western night in August 2003, I had my first night of class. I walked into the building, found my classroom, and sat on the front row, pencil and paper in hand, eager not to miss anything. And that first class, I was introduced to Stephen Brookfield, Jack Mezirow, and John Dewey with their theory about critical thinking and making meaning from a lived experience through self-reflection.

I was 32 years old and had plenty of life experience to contribute to my ever-evolving perspective. I had no idea that my lived experience would contribute to what I would learn in class. After I turned in my first college assignment and received positive feedback from my professor *(your writing is very poetic and informative)*, I became more confident in my ability to earn a four-year undergraduate degree, which I planned to complete — no matter what.

Before long, I finished my first eight-week term, earned an "A," and this accomplishment motivated me to reach my projected graduation date of May 2005. The next eight-week term came around, and before I knew it, I was on holiday break. I loved being back in school.

But would you believe that in January 2004, I discovered I was pregnant for a second time? However, I was stronger mentally and physically with this second pregnancy, and I saw the light at the end of my educational tunnel. I was joyful at the reality of becoming a mother again. In the past, I quickly became discouraged when I faced an obstacle and withdrew whenever I felt like it was too much to handle. But this time, I was determined to continue my education and was prepared to bring both of my babies to class, if necessary. Although my second pregnancy was normal in every way, what happened after the baby was delivered had everybody scratching their head.

Remember, my first child was breeching the entire pregnancy, and I had no choice but to have a Cesarean delivery. Meanwhile, throughout my doctor's visits with my second pregnancy, my obstetrician tried to convince me to have a vaginal delivery because the baby was in the correct delivery position. But that was not what I wanted. I wanted to have another C-section.

The closer I got to my due date, the more I wanted to have a C-section. I even had nightmares of having a vaginal delivery and something going terribly wrong. My spirit would not rest; every fiber in my being told me to have another C-section.

I wrote in my journal sporadically during this time. I still had a very active toddler who demanded my attention, plus I was back in school, so at night I would collapse into bed without making time to write in my journal. But the closer I got to my delivery date, the more I became prompted to jot some things down. My routine may have changed over time, but my approach didn't. I still kept a journal and pen by my bedside.

8/24/2004

Today's doctor visit went well. The baby's head is completely engaged, and I've dropped considerably; however, no dilation. The doctor predicts another two or three weeks. Once again, I tried to talk to him about a C-section and he ain't trying to hear me. He brushed off my request and said that nothing can be scheduled until a week before estimated delivery date. Ultimately, the decision is the baby's, with the help of the Almighty! So, I must enjoy these golden days of pregnancy as the end is soon approaching. I'm excited, anxious, and nervous all at the same time. I know I should not have any fear but a part of me can't help it. I pray for things to go smoothly yet everything is so unpredictable.

I know that this delivery will be altogether different than the first time — but how? My prayer is that we will remain healthy. I want my baby to be healthy and happy! I'm excited to see my sweet little baby's face. Lord, help me to relax and know that YOU will take care of both of us. 176lbs. Lord, give me strength and peace. I completed my last class of the term tonight. Thank you, Jesus!

So, it was the first Tuesday in September 2004 that I went into labor. I actually labored the entire Labor Day weekend and didn't fully realize it. Remember, with my first pregnancy, I arrived at the hospital and eased into labor with the help of medication in my veins because the baby was still breech, and the operating room was just across the hall. I felt no pain with that delivery, only suffered an infection of my uterus after I was discharged and was admitted back into the hospital for three days of treatment.

My second pregnancy was entirely different. The night before I delivered my baby, I hardly slept — partly because my belly was so large that I could not get comfortable, but also because I kept feeling the urge to urinate only to wobble to the bathroom, and only a trickle would come out. By the time the morning came, and my daughter was fully awake and active, I wobbled around the house in an oversized shirt and no pants because I was tired of struggling to pull them up and down when I got to the bathroom. In addition to the constant urge to pee, I had waves of pain in my belly, butt, and back. These waves of pain stopped me in my tracks. I called my doctor, and since my water had not broken, I was told to take it easy and come to the hospital if things got worse. Worse? As far as I knew, things were worse, but it was only the beginning.

Instinctively, I began to nest and do laundry, dishes and take care of my daughter between the waves of pain. I even took the dog for a short walk. I was home alone. By the time I put my daughter down for a nap, I had flopped in the rocking chair in her room and began to pray. I rocked back and forth, and the only words I could mutter were, "Jesus."

I repeated, "Jesus, Jesus, Jesus" each time I had a wave of pain. At the time, I did not know the power in that name and that whenever I uttered the name of Jesus, I was calling healing into my body.

That evening, my husband came home, and I met him at the door for him to take me to the hospital. It was the most uncomfortable ride of my life. I tried to sit on my side hip because every bump made me feel like I would poop myself. When I arrived at the hospital, I was informed that my obstetrician was on vacation and his partner would take all of his patients. Once in a Labor and Delivery room, the new doctor introduced himself and asked me a straightforward question, "How are we going to bring this baby into the world?" Without hesitation, I responded, "C-section." Next, he announced to me and instructed the nurses to hurry and get me ready for a C-section; otherwise, the baby would enter this world on its own, whether we liked it or not.

The C-section was a success, and I delivered a screaming, healthy baby boy. But after delivery, the energy of the operating room shifted. When I was brought into the operating room before delivery, the medical staff all chatted about their weekend and asked me questions about my soon-to-be-born baby, like what names I had picked out and how I spent my weekend.

But after the baby was delivered (screaming and crying as expected) and was handed over to the pediatric staff, the operating room became unnaturally quiet. Eerily quiet. Only the sounds of the machines filled the empty space where laughter and chatter once occupied. I was familiar with a C-section delivery process since my daughter was born just twenty-two months prior. I knew what to expect, but when two hours had passed and I was still on the operating table with the only sound in the room coming from the machines, I knew something was wrong.

After my son was lifted out of my womb, the doctors had to repair tissue on my bladder because the baby pushed as far as he could and created significant damage to my bladder. This explained why I had no bladder control the entire day. The doctors also noticed what they thought was a cyst on my left ovary, but once drained of its fluid, there was "oddly-shaped, discolored" tissue underneath. This issue presented a problem for everybody because I was there to deliver a baby and nothing else. After the lead doctor got me to what he felt was a safe zone, he came and sat on a stool next to my head. Keep in mind that I was only numb from the waist down, so I was fully alert. He explained that there were a few complications after my son was delivered that caused them to take so long, and he told me about the bladder issue.

Next, he told me about the cyst on my left ovary and the oddly shaped, discolored tissue underneath. A portion of that tissue was removed and sent to pathology for further testing. The doctor talked to me with the surgical mask over his mouth. Although I heard every word he said, his eyes told a different story. At some point, he pulled down his surgical mask and assured me that everything would be okay. My recovery might take a little longer, but I would be okay. He then congratulated me on the delivery of my son and announced that I would soon be moved to the recovery room. He smiled, stood up, turned to exit the operating room, and removed his gloves.

After he made his exit, the room went back to silence with only the sounds of the machines. As the nursing staff wheeled my bed out of the operating room and into a recovery room, I noticed several extra-large yellow biohazard bags lined against the wall, all filled with bright red bloody gauze that came from me. I was scared.

The next day, test results came back and proved the tissue malignant, and I was caught between joy and pain, happiness and confusion. Once again, depression hovered and hung on me like a cold, wet blanket. I went from a team of obstetricians to a team of oncologists. I stayed in the hospital five days after delivery because the doctors did not know what to do with me. My case was a mystery. Do they keep me in the hospital and prepare for a partial (or full) hysterectomy, or do they let me go home, bond with my baby, and THEN bring me back for additional surgery?

Each day it seemed like a new person from the oncology team came into my room to explain the various scenarios. I saw their mouth move, but the sounds I heard sounded like a scene from a Charlie Brown episode. I could not focus on the possible outcomes of another surgery. Instead, I focused my energy on the vibrant life of my newborn son. I made peace with whatever the outcome would be. I completely surrendered it all to God. I was at the full mercy of God and HIS will for my life.

After I was finally discharged from delivering my second child and was back at home, I used all of my strength to enjoy the bursting energy of my newborn son and my daughter, who was now a toddler. Unlike his big sister, my son had no problem latching onto my breast. He latched on so tight and nursed with such force that I could not keep up with his demand for food.

This was something I was not made aware of by a parenting book. But I decided to feed my son formula from a bottle. And this choice worked well because a few weeks after delivery, Cookie came for a visit and to help with the kids, which gave me a chance to experience a side of her I had never witnessed before. I saw how she was somewhat nurturing and loving to her two grandchildren. Sure, the kids might have had on their diapers longer than usual, and I needed to lift and change a toddler even though I was on full restriction not to lift anything, Cookie did better with my children than I ever expected. I was glad that we had the time to share and get somewhat reconnected. But it was still hard to be around her, so I remained guarded and anxious.

Meanwhile, when I wasn't feeding and changing my children, I read the Bible and encouraged myself to remain strong, no matter the outcome of my upcoming surgery. I wrote Scripture verses on notecards and placed them around the house where I could see them all the time. In the children's room, next to the changing table, in the kitchen, next to the bottle warmer, in the bathroom, and on my bedside table. I was starved for affection, comfort, and compassion. My children were the only true empathetic energy source I could draw from. I didn't have much strength during this time, but what strength I did have, I devoted to my children and my faith. Nevertheless, seven weeks after my son was born, I returned to the hospital and had laparoscopic surgery to remove my left ovary and fallopian tube.

The surgery was a success, and no further treatment was necessary. But at some point, while I was in the hospital, directly after my laparoscopic surgery, I woke from the fog of the anesthesia, and thought I died, went to heaven, and saw Brett Favre. It was the fall of 2004 in Wisconsin, and Brett Favre was a football god to all who loved the Green Bay Packers. Once I finally became clear in my thoughts, I realized that a life-sized cutout of Brett Favre stood in the corner of the hospital recovery room. As nurses discharged me and wheeled me past the larger-than-life cutout, I laughed at myself and blew a kiss to my guardian angel. My future was bright, and I was on my way to a full recovery.

Despite the favorable prognosis, recovery was painful and difficult. To make things even more complicated, I suffered postpartum depression. This time, I recognized that my tears were more attached to sadness instead of grief, like when Mama Pauline passed away and I had my daughter. At a postpartum visit, I talked to my doctor about my feelings of sadness and moments when I cried for no reason. I also spoke to him about my family history of depression and my personal battle. He prescribed an antidepressant that helped me cope. It was a rough journey parenting two small children and living in the harsh, blustery weather of the mid-west, but five days after my laparoscopic surgery, I returned to class more determined than ever to complete my bachelor's degree.

CHAPTER 10

Good Choice

> "Even strong young lions sometimes go hungry, but those of us who reverence the Lord will never lack any good thing."
> —Psalm 34:10

WHEN I DISCOVERED THAT I was pregnant for a second time, I immediately scheduled an appointment with my college advisor and registered to take two classes per week, instead of one. The new class schedule allowed me to stay on track with completing my core classes plus add an elective. Although I had a passion for writing, I had never taken a formal writing class. I signed up for a creative writing course, and this introduced me to writing workshops and the various writing genres. With the encouragement of my writing professor, I entered a poetry slam contest held at a local festival that was open to the public.

I had never read any of my poems in public, neither had any of my poems judged by esteemed writers and the Wisconsin Poet Laureate. There were maybe twenty participants, and at the end, there was a three-way tie. I was one of the three. We all performed our poems again and waited for the result — it was something out of an American Idol episode. I walked away with the third-place winnings: $10

But so many times, I felt overwhelmed by everything. I was at home with the children during the day and taking two classes a week at night. Sleep was a luxury I did not have. I could only focus on my schoolwork after the kids were bathed and put to bed. And this meant that I would be up till way after midnight only to get up at dawn to let the dog out and feed the babies. This cycle ran in a continuous loop for eight weeks. I was beyond exhausted.

03/08/2005

I honestly don't know how I am going to make it and get everything done. Today, she has used the potty three times... and he has started to crawl. I can't keep up with everything. All I want to do is sleep.

04/24/2005

Lord, please give me strength! For there are times that I certainly feel I can't make it... things are moving fast. My babies are growing up. Thank you, Jesus, for this day.

And it was with all that prayer and all that faith that in May 2005, I earned my Bachelor of Arts degree from Ottawa University. I made straight A's throughout the program, except for one "B" from a class I had taken right before delivering my son. Nevertheless, it was a dream come true for me to have my four-year degree. The faculty voted me to be one of the student speakers at the commencement ceremony. In my speech, I shared how the decision to return to school required me to have faith and determination to overcome many challenges and achieve my goals. I maintained good relationships with all faculty and staff even after graduating and was asked to be a participant on several panels to share my experience with potential students. And I loved everything about sharing my story and inspiring others to complete their educational goals.

After I graduated with my Bachelor of Arts degree in Management with a concentration in Communication from Ottawa University, I felt bored. Yes, I was a full-time mother of two children . . . but what was next. I longed for more.

06/05/2005

Big sigh as I fall into bed. Boy, am I exhausted. I just completed a marathon. I bathed the kids, changed the sheets on all the beds, dishes, laundry, garbage out, walked dog, cleaned carpets, cooked, showered, killed a fly... now I'm finally in bed ready for a good night's sleep. I pray for peaceful sleep with pleasant dreams. Thank you, Jesus!

But I missed being in the classroom and learning new things.

06/30/2005

I feel myself on the edge of a breakdown... The only freedom I have is in the classroom.

I still struggled with postpartum depression, and it seemed to flare up even worse now that I wasn't in school anymore. When I was in school, I felt empowered, like I made a meaningful contribution by reading, writing, researching, and discussing complex issues with other people. But after I graduated, I went back to being isolated in my suburban, all-White neighborhood.

The rugged, mid-western winter only intensified the loneliness since I was no longer in school. Winter showed up early in Wisconsin and stayed late. I still turned to writing as my outlet and used every free moment to capture my innermost thoughts.

> **08/24/2005**
> Never have I experienced isolation and loneliness like I have here, and like I do in this very moment. Tears stream down my face as I write this. I cried while doing the dishes, vacuuming the rug, mopping the floor. Lord, please I beg you to save me. Save me from myself... I'm surrounded by the joy, innocence and curiosity of my children. Yet, I find it hard to enjoy because I'm sick of this cold place. I try my best to be strong for them to put on a happy face for them, but I can't. As much as I tried to hide it she saw my crying earlier. She ran to my side, "What's wrong, Mommy?" Her eyes became sad, her little hand touching my leg. Lord, help me to be strong for my children.

But on the same day that I had this breakdown, I received a call from Ottawa University Arizona campus. They had a copy of my commencement speech and wanted to expand their coverage into a feature article in their university publication and asked to conduct a phone interview with me for the article. I got off the phone, my tears dried up, and my soul felt lifted. As I retold my story, I felt empowered, but above anything, I felt blessed. For the first time, I felt that if my story could bring even one person closer to achieving their goal, then my purpose and passion had been fulfilled. Nobody could tell my story but me.

By the fall of 2005, I was invited to attend a local mega-church with a program designed for mothers with young children called Mothers of Preschoolers (MOPS). I attended a few sessions and was assigned to a small group of women to study the Bible teachings of Jesus. While I attended my class, my children went to their age-appropriate Bible class. It was a great time of teaching and fellowship. Before and after each meeting, there were refreshments.

The friend who invited me was part of the hospitality ministry, and instinctively I worked alongside her, helping to set up, clean, and organize the snack area. After a few weeks of simply doing what I always did — jump in and lend a hand. One of the ladies, who was in a leadership position, appreciated how willing I was to help set up and break down the snack area and recognized that I had a heart for service. She approached me to ask if I wanted to be part of the leadership team and invited me to an informational meeting. But would you believe that some of the moms took issue with how someone so new to the program, like me, could so easily be moved up the ranks?

It was one of the largest churches in the area, with hundreds of members, and this mom's program had plenty of suburban stay-at-home mothers who wished to be selected for a leadership role. Yet, I had only attended the program a few times and was asked immediately – plus, I was the only Black mother in the entire program with my little Black children running around learning about

Jesus, eating snacks, and making friends. Nevertheless, I accepted the offer, attended the leadership training, and became a prayer ministry leader — leading discussions among the group, taking prayer requests, and lifting them up to God on behalf of others.

This alone helped to set my spiritual life in the right direction. I prayed and meditated regularly, and this position took my spiritual habit of reading the Bible and praying to a new level. I carried notecards filled with handwritten Scriptures in my diaper bag, and my faith and hope grew as I began to understand that yes, I was a mom who had survived a cancer scare, but there were other mothers who dealt with situations worse than mine. This experience helped me to become more hopeful in many ways, both for myself and for others. I found that gratitude and appreciation was the best attitude no matter what. I prayed about everything and everybody.

After I finally graduated with my bachelor's degree, I felt a bit lost without school. For the first time, the classroom had given me a place where I felt like I belonged. As an adult, I had finally found a place to learn, share and grow. I could not shake this feeling of going to the next level. Therefore, I enrolled in graduate school and started my 2006 spring semester at Carroll University in their Master of Education program.

It was smack in the middle of a Midwest winter, and I needed something to save me because I was in crisis mode and needed to feed the fire that burned in my soul. And graduate school was my answer.

On the night of graduate orientation, my husband had to work late, so I had to take my children to the traditional campus setting with me. They were both extremely active at this time, and I prayed for full cooperation so that I could get the information I needed and get back home before all hell broke loose. My daughter was at the age where she could walk alongside me and hold my hand, but I had to tote my infant son in a car seat carrier, which was heavy. I sat in the back of the room where I could easily get to cookies and juice to feed the children, but I couldn't really hear all the information that was shared, and it didn't take long for me to become easily annoyed. I was not the only Black woman in the room, as was routine, but I was the only person who brought their young children to a college orientation event.

The other Black woman stood on the opposite side of the room and lovingly looked over at me with a knowing smile. But my children were fidgety, and they had gotten bored with the cookies. So, I hastily gathered them up, grabbed a graduate student orientation folder, and walked out. As I drove home, Smokie Norful's song, "I Understand," played on the CD player. I cried openly, doubting my foolish thoughts of believing that I could go to graduate school with two small children.

Once we arrived at the house, I put everybody to bed, and then grabbed a pen to scribble out my frustration.

01/13/2006

I'm spent, finished, out of fresh ideas, ready to throw my hands in the air. The main culprit, exhaustion. I'm tired of being the maid, cook, referee, doctor, lawyer, educator, fixer, healer, laundry lady, dog feeder, diaper changer, boo-boo cleaner, bottom wiper, milk-getter, entertainer, bather, clothier, story reader, disciplinarian, lover, thinker, doer... I feel like I'm in this all by myself. A married, single parent. I have to do it all, all the time! Plus, I hate this cold ass weather.

Nevertheless, at the end of January 2006, I began graduate classes. I was excited, motivated, and determined to get my master's degree. But exhaustion caught up with me around March when my husband had a 30-day overseas deployment, which left me in the throes of motherhood with no sleep while I juggled being back in school.

The Master of Education program challenged my thinking in new ways. Deep discussions about complex global issues prompted me to think outside the box, both uncomfortable and liberating. But, I couldn't articulate the shift that took place in my mind. It felt like something was happening *to me* and *through me* all at the same time. After I completed my spring semester, I took classes the following summer. Whatever was happening, I couldn't explain it, but I didn't want it to stop either, even when I felt weary, exhausted, and overwhelmed.

09/12/2006

I'm feeling completely overwhelmed — but I'm here. At this very moment, I wonder how I will get it all done — but I'm here. My head hurts — but I'm here. The fall semester has started, and I am taking three classes (nine graduate hours). Two words can best describe right now: Intense and Fruitful. *Intense* because it is a lot of work. *Fruitful* because I know in the end it will all pay off and this is just part of the process. Count it all Joy... even in my tests. Count it all Joy!

As I got deeper into the graduate level of learning, I made more connections between my life experiences and research theories. In turn, I felt more in control of my life in ways that I never experienced before. My mindset was in full transformation mode. I started to see and understand things differently. Under such a heavy inner transition, I decided that I wanted my outer appearance to reflect the changes. So, I started to cut my hair short. With an active school schedule and two active children, my hairstyle was the last thing I wanted to be concerned about.

Meanwhile, my home life turned into a different learning experience because it was during this time that my husband's job became even more demanding.

The military unit he was assigned to deployed to the Middle East, but he remained in the United States to cover other responsibilities. Part of his task was the unfortunate duty of notifying families when there was a casualty. Even with this obligation, he still kept the children while I attended classes in the evenings, or I had a babysitter on standby if he was unavailable. But the closer I came to completing my graduate degree, the more my husband contemplated retirement from the military.

At this point, he had over 20 years of active duty service. So, I went on the fast track and registered for three graduate-level classes in one semester because I wanted to complete my master's thesis before we relocated one final time. Everything happened all at once without a lot of time to pause, reflect and connect.

I spent every free moment I had at the university library. I was on campus at the library in the evenings, after class, and on the weekends. No amount of snow on the ground kept me away from campus, just being in the college atmosphere was enough to fuel my motivation to burn the midnight oil and complete my academic goals. This was in direct contrast to my earlier college experience as a student at Western Kentucky University. I kept an open line of communication with all of my professors and let them know the goals I had set and what obstacles I faced.

Dr. Robinson became my strongest supporter and ally at Carroll University. As the only Black professor in the Education department, by this time, she had been at the university for several years and knew the ins and outs of adult education. But more than that, she knew about life — the struggle and the triumph of being an educated Black woman. She grew up in the South, so she also knew about the movement. She participated in the Civil Rights Movement and completed her undergraduate studies at Howard University. She told me that when I walked into her office that first day, she saw a version of herself. She saw a woman with a story who was strong and determined to create a new path.

Dr. Robinson was the other Black woman in the room at the graduate orientation. She remembered seeing me there struggling with two small children and knew that I was determined to make it all work. In the end, Dr. Robinson became the guiding force of wisdom and knowledge that I desperately needed. She became more than a professor, more than a mentor. Even when I stayed after class with additional questions after a discussion, she became the voice of discernment to help me further process and analyze information. When I felt exhausted and lost focus, she became the loudest cheerleader when I completed a goal.

I would not have made it through the graduate program without Dr. Robinson and her guidance. I would come home from class and be so charged up that it would take a while for me to settle in and drift off to sleep. In those moments, I would get in bed to rest my body, and I would write in my journal to clear my mind.

Energy from sources unknown helped me to power through a heavy graduate course load at Carroll University. It was the first time I had been on a traditional college campus since 1990 at Western Kentucky University. My motivation and mindset were completely different. Meanwhile, motherhood started to level out a bit, and I began to enjoy parenting two high-spirited toddlers. I also began to thrive in graduate school and this new dimension of learning. So, one cold February day in 2006, Dr. Robinson had a conversation with me about my future. She asked me to stay after class and told me how I should apply to a doctoral program, and recommended that I do it now and not later. Dr. Robinson knew it would not be easy for me and offered to be available to support me because a solid support system was vital.

Next, she looked me in the eye and said, "We need sharp people to get things done and bridge those gaps. For some people, it is a struggle. For you, it is a gift. When you find a job, let that be a means, not an end. You need to go for your doctorate. I am here to support you. You can do it!" After our conversation, I started to research doctoral programs and printed off a checklist of the steps I needed to take. Dr. Robinson had a lot of confidence in me, and I was deeply grateful for her guidance.

10/30/2006

Dr. Robinson and I talked at great length tonight about my future in the graduate program. She encouraged me to begin my master's thesis NOW – before January. I appreciated her input and confidence in me. She selected me to be the liaison between her and Dr. Edwards, as we prepared for his visit to campus. Thank you, Jesus, for opportunity. Thank you, Lord, for placing Dr. Robinson in my life.

By March 2006, I earned the Black Student Union Essay Scholarship. I organized and planned networking events to bring the university and the community together to provide services to students and families. I volunteered at schools and received requests to speak to students about my story and the importance of writing in a journal. During my talks, I noticed a few students with tears in their eyes when I shared about my early education days of being bullied. After one of my talks, a student approached me and said, "Your story inspired me. You should write a book."

One of the final assignments for my graduate class was to facilitate a discussion for ninety minutes. Each student was graded on specific facilitation techniques. It was 2007, and the movie "Crash" was a buzz. I watched and was compelled by all the complexities of every character and the storyline that weaved through the film of assumption, bias, racism, corruption, etc. I designed a movie screening that highlighted scenes to spark discussion about social injustice. I prepared resources, refreshments, and discussion questions for the audience to do a deep dive in their reflections and compare to certain movie scenes. I posted fliers around the campus, inviting the public to participate in the discussion.

It was my first time leading a discussion about complex issues. I was nervous. But once participants arrived, the clock started, and Dr. Robinson was in place with a clipboard and observation sheet ready to grade my every move. My nervousness quickly gave way to excitement. I got into a zone, posing questions to prompt critical thinking and challenging the audience to focus on similarities and not differences with every individual they came in contact with. Once the talk was over, I felt on top of the world and knew that I had found my calling to transform the way people think through information and inspiration. I passed my class, and "Crash" went on to win an Oscar that same year.

Meanwhile, I remained on the fast track with my classes and continued to take additional courses during the summer. I even took the initiative and coordinated a networking holiday event at the university president's house. No time off. All school. All parenting. All full steam ahead. All the semesters started to blend, and the next thing I knew, I was selected to receive the 2008 Excellence in Education Graduate Program Award.

Somehow, all the blustery winter days in the college library, summer school, and late nights paid off because, on a Monday in March 2008, I completed my graduate research and presented my master's thesis to my committee and my classmates. By the following Wednesday, I received my final grade for my last class.

The entire education department knew about my situation and was more than willing to support my fast track to complete the program before the spring semester's official end. So, I finished in the middle of the semester and attended the graduation ceremony on May 11, 2008, to officially receive my Master of Education degree to focus on Adult and Continuing Education from Carroll University.

This fast track to my graduate school completion was because back in March of that same year, my husband retired from the military the same week I completed my master's research.

His retirement ceremony was an elaborate event that included a declaration from the city mayor. By mid-March 2008, after receiving my final grades, we loaded up the mini-van and drove to Kentucky to move into the new five-bedroom house we just purchased.

It was a full-circle moment for me because it had been ten years since I had left Kentucky and moved to Hawaii. But with several major life events to happen all at once, my stress level skyrocketed. Two weeks before my husband's military retirement ceremony, I bought a new pantsuit. On the day of the ceremony, I got dressed, and the pants literally fell off my waist. I was rapidly losing weight . . . and I also felt like I was slowly losing my mind.

Achieving

CHAPTER 11

Good Transition

> "For the Lord your God is bringing you into a good land
> of brooks, pools, gushing springs, valleys, and hills."
> –Deuteronomy 8:7

T HE YEAR WAS 2008, and by this time, I had lived away from my home state for a decade. A lot had changed. Even though I had always visited Kentucky, after I married and moved away, living back in my hometown was a hard adjustment for me. I did not count on feeling lost in a place that was once so familiar. I cried behind tinted glasses as I drove down the street where I grew up. The small house on Clay Street that once provided so much love, safety, and security, was now home to another family. The energy of everything felt odd and heavy.

Once, I visited the local nursing home to see a family friend and was immediately flooded with memories of my last visit when Mama Pauline had been a resident. The smell of the facility triggered up emotions I was not ready to face, and I had a complete mental breakdown filled with grief, anxiety, depression, exhaustion, and loneliness. I became a stranger in my hometown. A new level of depression consumed me. I could do nothing, so I surrendered to the process and trusted God to bring me through. I purged. It was a critical period in my development, and although I found myself sitting silent a lot of times, I knew I was on the verge of a big transition. So in between the tears, I wrote in my journal.

06/20/2008

I literally don't know who I am right now. I look in the mirror and see a shell. I wander around this big house aimlessly — not really knowing what to do. It's almost as if I've disappeared and something/someone else is occupying my space. I zombie around doing all the routine stuff like a machine or robot. I need something constructive to occupy my mind because my mind is being occupied by other things — troubling things. I need help. I need someone to help me — help ME. If I'm half the person I was before I earned my master's, then I don't know who I am now that I have completed it. I shopped for clothes the other day... I wear a size 2! WTF!

I don't remember how I parented the children at this time. I can only recall that I felt lost, alone and lonely. I cried every day.

Eventually, I reached out to Dr. Robinson. Although I was no longer her student and lived in a different state, I still longed for her guidance. When I told her my current mindset, her advice was simple. She told me to learn to love myself. Love me? How do I do that? I had the capacity and ability to love and take care of everyone else, but I didn't know what it required of me to love myself. Why was this simple task so hard?

In the fall of 2008, my daughter entered kindergarten, my son went to preschool, and I returned to full-time work at Kentucky State University. Kentucky's premier Historically Black College/University. This was my first full-time job since I earned my bachelor's and master's degrees. Additionally, I picked up a part-time job and taught at two different universities as an Adjunct. The only way I knew to cope was to stay busy. Exhaustion carried me from one task to the next.

Now that my husband was retired and I had graduated, we struggled to embrace each other in our new life chapters. But old patterns in behavior continued to show up in our relationship. We grew distant and operated out of comfort and convenience.

> **06/01/2008**
> ...silent treatment ...lack of understanding.

When I had decided to get married, I assumed that he saw marriage the same way I did. I saw marriage as a whole and complete commitment with no room for anything or anyone else. I saw marriage as an opportunity to cut off any loose ends with past relationships to make room for a new future filled with loyalty, honesty, and friendship. But I was the only one in the relationship with these expectations. I was the only one in the relationship who severed all ties to any old acquaintances who could potentially contaminate my marriage.

Before I moved to Hawaii, I purged and destroyed all pictures, cards, notes, etc., that were attached to any old boyfriend or random hook-up. I even threw away all of my old VHS pornographic videotapes. Meanwhile, no one ever had a clear conversation with me about marriage. Therefore, I never had a clear conversation with my husband early on about my expectations. So, I acted on my assumptions of what I thought marriage should be, and I did what I thought was right.

Cookie never married, and the only marriage model for me was my Great-grandparents, who were from a completely different generation. Mama Pauline was sixteen, and Daddy Boots was eighteen when they got married, right before The Great Depression, and they stayed married until death. By the time Mama and Daddy started taking care of me, they were in their mid-fifties. I never saw them argue. While Daddy worked multiple jobs and his paychecks provided for the family's physical needs, Mama worked inside the home. Her nurturing and compassionate spirit supplied the emotional needs of the family.

This was the framework of marriage that I had around me. I expected my marriage to fall into the same frame, but I never clearly communicated this expectation to my husband – nor did I ever ask about his marriage expectation. I only assumed, and every assumption creates conflict.

Over the years, we shared some good times, especially those early years. I kept every letter he wrote me while he was overseas. And I missed him deeply when he was away.

But over the years, we found ourselves on a collision course, and more and more, we simply settled for a life of parenting our children and occupying the same dwelling. The intimacy was gone, and we became complacent. And for all the wrong reasons, I turned to the old habit of alcohol to cope. I isolated myself from family and friends and fell into a routine of going to work, coming home, and putting the kids to bed.

Each of my jobs gave me college-level teaching experience, so I was somewhat happy to finally build a career in higher education and make my own money, but something was still missing. I kept thinking to myself, "there has got to be a better way!" Then something beyond my control nudged me to go to the next level. And I began to entertain the idea of going back to school to earn my doctoral degree.

As I mentioned earlier, as a high school student, the idea of college was never my goal. My only priority was to get my high school diploma and get as far away from Kentucky as I could, and I did when I moved to Texas. Now, I was back in Kentucky, raising my family and contemplating returning to school to earn my doctorate. The only reason I ever went to college in the first place was that my good friend Allison encouraged me to give it a try. For every college course I passed, Allison was in the back of my mind. I even dedicated my master's thesis to her. I felt like her spirit guided me on that educational journey. And even though Dr. Robinson encouraged me to apply for a doctoral program before I completed my master's degree, I never really pursued it beyond printing off a doctoral completion checklist. My life had been a whirlwind for the past year and a half.

I remembered that as a kid, my favorite movie to watch with Allison was *The Wizard of Oz*. We were both scared of the lion but also appreciated his courage. As we grew older, we laughed at our fear of the lion because he was afraid of the unknown, but he discovered there was nothing to be afraid of if he kept moving forward. The idea of going back to school to earn a doctoral degree filled me with fear and anxiety. Yet, there was something beyond my control that pushed me toward this new educational endeavor. So, in September 2009, at 38 years old, I enrolled in the Doctor of Education program of study at Walden University — a fully online doctoral program.

When I initially explored doctoral plans, I needed to build on the master's degree I had already earned. I searched all the universities in my area, and not one of them had the program I desired. Online learning was fresh and new, and I found a program that partnered well with my interest and background. Nevertheless, online learning came with a new level of excitement and anxiety. I felt anxious because this would be my first time taking online classes. Until this point, I took courses on campus, in a face-to-face format, with other students and a professor. In the past, if I had a question or needed extra help understanding a concept or theory, I had quick face-to-face access to someone who could point me in the right direction.

In my master's program, a cohort was formed to provide accountability, collaboration, and support. We often met after class and on weekends, pending the project, and analyzed or discussed research. We supported each other. Meanwhile, I was entirely on my own in the online doctoral program. And in that space, I reflected on my journey and continued to capture my thoughts in my journal.

> **10/25/2009**
> Thank you, Lord, for bringing me through. For some reason, I can't help but think of the time I spent in Texas, and how that was such a pivotal point in my life. It was a gut-wrenching experience, yet one that truly turned my life around... Lord, thank you for taking me in and bringing me out. Thank you for the hurt, the pain, the scars and tears. Thanks for my life and for wisdom. Thank you, Lord, for bringing me through because without these experiences I wouldn't be where I am now.

The Doctor of Education curriculum was intense, and the online format was demanding. Although I formed friendships with classmates via the discussion board, emails, and phone calls, it did not take the place of the authentic face-to-face connection I was used to.

I was a first-generation doctoral student and leaned very heavily on the knowledge and skills acquired from my master's degree to help me get through. I kept an active membership to professional organizations, took advantage of the student rate, and presented at national and international conferences. Even though I was overwhelmed with work and school, I welcomed every opportunity to be around like-minded people.

Late November 2009, I presented my first roundtable discussion at an international conference held in Cleveland, Ohio. I was super excited to share my research on the value of reflective journals to promote transformative learning. My roundtable was packed, and some even pulled chairs from other areas to gather around and hear what I shared. Later in the conference, I was in the elevator, and a gentleman told me that he enjoyed hearing my story and learning about my research. I became excited at his excitement. The scholarly environment gave me new insight and energy to move forward in what I wanted to do in a career and life. I needed this bright light because other areas of my life were very dark.

My full-time job at the HBCU became a toxic work environment, and I welcomed the healthy distraction of being a student again to work on a doctoral degree.

Life at home had also become a toxic environment because my husband and I had fallen into the routine of passive-aggressive behavior towards one another. This pattern was established from the beginning — not seeing, listening, or being fully present with the other person. Throughout the marriage, I turned to my journal because it was the only place where I felt I had a voice.

> **04/25/1999**
> We have gotten along a little better this week and I'm glad.

> **04/26/1999**
> I wish things were better. I wish he understood. I wish he was more patient...

12/27/2000

It was our anniversary four days ago. Now we have hardly said two words to each other in the past twenty-four hours. This habit, as foolish as it is, has become easier and easier for us. We ignore each other for no apparent reason.

12/31/2000

It's the eve of a new year and people are popping champagne to toast in a new year. And here I lay in the bed of our guest bedroom writing this entry. He is on the couch in the living room watching T.V. Something he has done for the past three days. We still barely talk. I've tried every attempt to break the tension to open the lines of communication, but to no avail. He acts as if I don't exist... like I'm not even here. How did it come to this? Five whole days... it has never gone this long. We had sex yesterday and it was intense but no real connection. But soon after, the silence resumed, and he hasn't touched or talked to me since. Lord, please give me peace. Lord, please give me harmony.

05/05/2005

Speak the wrong words. Ears burn from the sound. I can't stand the silence. We are the ones in control. But we lose it. Habits are hard to break. I'm broken in a million pieces. Only YOU Lord can put me back together again. I put all of my trust in YOU!

> **06/23/2006**
> I keep holding my breath waiting for things to get better, waiting to be first, waiting to be taken over by harmony, happiness, and peace.

> **01/04/2007**
> "Couples go through this type of shit all the time. Everybody doesn't get along all the time. I don't know what type of books you have been reading but if you think you are going to have a relationship that is nothing but harmony ALL THE TIME, you need to think again. This is life. Couples don't always get along."

I bought into his way of thinking and seeing our relationship for a long time. But I kept holding out, hoping, praying that things would get better. Everything — and everyone — was always more important than we were to each other.

After the children got older, we continued this dysfunctional habit, and we talked to each other by not talking or talking through the children. "Ask your mother if…." or "Go see if your father is ready for…" and the other person would be sitting just across the room within earshot. There were no deep, meaningful, heartfelt conversations about anything, just denial, deflection, and blame.

The marital intimacy was in decline and had been for a while. So, once again, I shifted my focus to two things that brought me the most joy, my children and school. I turned up my energy to make my projected doctoral degree completion date of fall 2012.

I felt good about my choice to return to school and was on the right path to take my education to the next level. I had taken the risk knowing full well that the journey would not be easy, but I was on my way to becoming a doctor, something I never imagined I would be. What could possibly happen now? I was on a path to growing my mind beyond limitations and did not want to fall back into old thinking or habits. My heart and mind longed for something more, but I still felt stuck.

CHAPTER 12

Good Trip

> "The good man wins his case by careful argument; the evil-minded only wants to fight." *- Proverbs 13:2*

BY THIS TIME, I had become familiar with my emotional patterns of being up one day and down the next, but I never really dwelled on it because I always had the children and school as a distraction. But this felt different. I fought through the suspicions in my head and bought into my limited belief that it was just something that couples went through and adjusted my mindset accordingly not to rock the boat. But a pen stayed in my hand, and a journal was always within reach, so I wrote my innermost feelings without holding anything back.

06/26/2010
I wish I knew what was going on with me. Is there something beyond depression? What I am feeling goes beyond the daily hell I report to and call a job, something is really going on that I can't fake

anymore. I have been numb for more than eight years, operating in a fog cloud often rushed, hurried with a gun-held-to-my-head-kind-of-way. I'm tired of talking about it. Tired of feeling this way. Tired of being surrounded by people who don't understand me.

Two weekends in a row I have binged only to pay the price the next day by not being able to function. Today is one of those days. I am in the bed now. I try my best with what I have, but still ain't enough. I'm stretched beyond measure, but still ain't enough. I have no idea how to get what I really want and still be okay. I'm a cloud of confusion, no direction dizzy from the circle I keep running in.

Lord, help me in this desperate time of need. Please put me back together again. Please!

In public, I appeared to be a success. I worked two jobs, was a parent of two children. I had earned multiple degrees (and was working on another one), a new home, and married more than a decade. But privately, I suffered a slow death.

I kept feeling on the verge of something but unsure what that something was, how to articulate it or how to get it. I left the house early and returned home late. My commute was insane. Once at home, with the few minutes I could steal to check in on the children, who were already asleep, I showered, stayed up way past midnight to grade papers and complete my homework assignments, then fell into bed . . . only to repeat the cycle over again. Plus, there were times that I still grieved for everything and everybody who were no longer in my hometown now that I was back there. But I couldn't find the time or space for any inner peace and stayed anxious.

I was a ticking time bomb on the inside. The year I turned thirty-nine, I reflected on how I felt at that moment.

> **09/29/2010**
> Yesterday was my birthday. Today I wish I was dead. I hate my life and everything in it.

The rest of 2010 was more of the same up and down roller coaster of emotions and energy. But by the end of that year, I became more focused on my doctoral studies and truly committed to a strong finish. I knew that 2011 would put me closer to completing that goal, and it would also be the year that I turned forty. I needed to get ready to embrace everything this new decade of life would bring me.

> **01/09/2011**
> This is it! This is my year. The year I turn 40! In just nine months, I will close out three decades of living and embrace a new one. I'm looking forward to it. In the meantime, in the last week, I have noticed changes in my body, like weight gain in my hips, butt, and belly sections. How do I know? Because all of my jeans are super-tight, even the ones that are not supposed to be are now hoochie-coo-tight. Damn, gotta start making some changes and get this figure in shape. Lord, give me motivation.

April had become a significant month for me, ever since Mama Pauline died, but it brought its joys and challenges. Here it was, nine years since she passed away, and I noticed a pattern that the month of April showed me love, like when I received the call to be a student speaker at Ottawa's 2005 commencement ceremony or when I facilitated the courageous conversation about the movie "Crash" (2007) in graduate school.

I still longed to be with Mama, to hear her voice, and get her guidance on parenting and other life challenges. Now that I lived back in my small town, I took flowers to her gravesite or sent balloons to heaven with a note from the kids attached.

Then, on April 20, 2011, something happened that filled me with joy and then punched me in the stomach and made me sick. At the end of March, I had received an official letter from Carroll University, the college where I earned my master's degree. The letter informed me that the faculty had invited me to be inducted into The Honor Society of Phi Kappa Phi. Admission to this prestigious honor society was by invitation only. Carroll University had newly formed a chapter on its campus, and I was invited in. An official induction ceremony was scheduled for April 20th. So, I booked a flight to depart Kentucky on April 19th, destination Wisconsin.

My husband booked his trip to arrive in Wisconsin a day before me. He scheduled his travel ahead of me so that he would have a full day to reconnect with old friends and golf. We would both attend my ceremony and then return to Kentucky together just before the Easter weekend. Cookie was available and stayed at our house and kept the children while we were away. Plus, she planned to stay for Easter, and my sister and her children were coming to Kentucky for the weekend, and we would all be together, something that had not happened in a very long time.

I arrived at the Louisville International airport for my afternoon flight. But the sky had turned dark and cloudy by mid-afternoon. I sat at the gate and watched as the clouds became darker and the winds picked up speed. Several hours went by before the airline announced that it would be canceling all flights due to extreme weather and a tornado warning.

The next and only scheduled flight to Wisconsin was the following evening, which would put me there after my honor society induction ceremony. I missed the event.

I was utterly crushed that I could not make the flight. And even more, I was devastated because I had high hopes that a trip back to Wisconsin would be just the break needed to help me feel accomplished and vibrant again. But it didn't happen, and I fell even deeper into my rabbit hole of despair.

04/20/2011

Lord, forgive me, but right now I am extremely-extremely disappointed, and I can't help but ask why? Why has this happened to me? Why does it seem like every attempt to make my situation better fails? Why do I keep hitting brick walls? Today, right now, I should be in Wisconsin getting initiated into The Honor Society of Phi Kappa Phi. Instead I am at home, pillow wet from the endless tears I keep crying.

Last night, my flight was cancelled due to extreme weather. Sure, not being on a plane in the middle of a thunderstorm/tornado probably saved my life, but waking up and realizing that my goal of networking and making connections with people who really know me and know what I am capable of will not happen, only makes me wish for death. I woke up and realized that I wanted to die, that death was better than going into that dreaded toxic place where I work and getting all the life sucked out of me. So why not just get it over with?

In my mind, going to WI, getting that award, being around like-minded people was what had kept me going and gave me some hope. It would get me noticed and connected to the right people who could possibly make some things happen for me. Instead all the wind is knocked out of me, all hope gone. Without hope, what's the use of a lifeless life? This is my pity-party. No one can relate or understand. It is what it is.

So, this is how things will play out. I will put on a fake face and pretend like everything is okay while being on the verge of tears and ready to cry at the drop of a hat. In my fakeness, I will need to numb the pain, so a drink will just do the trick. One drink will lead to another and more alcohol than I can handle will be in my system — before you know it — CRASH — but not before great embarrassment, shame, guilt, headache where I will stay in bed, lifeless only to rejuvenate enough to repeat my mind-numbing ritual.

The last thing I want is a house full of people, but that's what I will have. I just want to crawl in my dark place and be left alone. Completely alone. I'm not even motivated to get up and call the airline for my refund.

This victim "roller coaster" ride I was on continued for several days. I sincerely wanted to return to Wisconsin, where I had made such an impression on the world of academia as a graduate student because I needed to feel validated. When the trip was canceled, I spiraled into a "why me," "what about me," "nobody cares about me," victim mindset. And having Cookie in the house only added to my anxiety.

She had visited me on several occasions throughout my marriage. She even showed up for one visit when I asked her not to come when we lived in Washington, D.C., and she could make the trip from North Carolina in a few short hours. No matter how old I was or no matter how many children I had, when I got a visit from Cookie, I turned back into the five-year-old — anxious for her to arrive, only to be glad when the time came for her to leave after the honeymoon wore off.

It was an unconscious cycle that I couldn't get myself out of, plus she and my husband got along really well, so a lot of times when she visited, I retreated to the bed as a way to escape and let the two of them laugh, enjoy each other's company and play cards. But when Easter rolled around, what I thought would be a disaster of me faking it until I made it and having way too much to drink ended up being a good time with food, family, and fun.

04/24/2011

Today was Easter and it was a wonderful day. All the family gathered at my house and everyone had a lot of fun. There was no drama, just love and fellowship. There was an abundance of food. Thank you Lord for your provision. Thank you, Lord, for Your Son. Thank you, Lord, for family and new memories made. Continue to give me strength!

Meanwhile, the spring semester ended, and I picked up even more sections to teach as an online adjunct faculty member. This meant that I could maintain the same income level without the long commute or toxic work environment. To teach online allowed me to work from virtually anywhere and still stay on top of my doctoral assignments, which became more intense with each semester.

With this in mind, I decided to resign from my full-time job at the HBCU, which was hell on earth for me. Reporting to a place that did not value my ideas, suggestions and micro-managed every little thing I did was just the tip of the toxicity that I faced for the past three years. My mental health was in swift decline, and I needed to rescue myself before I went beyond where I could get help.

05/28/2011

I'm fighting back tears right now as I write this. I just want to cry. My reality makes me want to cry, right now. It's a holiday weekend and a long weekend. I even played hooky yesterday and now all I can think of is going back to hell on Tuesday. Dammit I feel so trapped that I can't even enjoy the freshness of a new day. Depression. I fight it daily, constantly. My entire life, I have been in this fight. I mask it well and even those closest to me wouldn't know. Nothing that a cold beer or a glass of bourbon don't help. But that's the temporary fix for a deeper problem, a serious problem that has plagued me for years. Depression. The more I deny it, the more I fight it. The more I try to cure myself, the more I know I need help. The more excuses that I make, the worse it gets. Lord, help me in this place. Lord, help me right where I am right now. Lord, I need a miracle and I need it right now! In Jesus name — help me now!

To add to my mounting anxiety and depression, my husband and I grew more distant, even if publicly we appeared to be a loving, adoring couple.

Very early in the marriage, we each acted in ways that were not becoming of two people who loved each other and fell into the habit of denial, deflection, and dysfunction. I looked for attention outside of our marriage, and so did he. The lack of accountability and responsibility could be blamed on both sides. Although these unhealthy behavior patterns were modeled for me before I married my husband, my heart desired something different. In the back of my mind, I told myself that there had to be a better way. I wanted to break the cycle.

When the demands of my husband's military life were over, I still did not receive the attention, patience, loyalty, and friendship I hoped I would get once he retired. I held out in hopes that things would get better. To make matters worse, I noticed patterns in my husband's behavior that I recognized from the past. This was the toxic relationship I was in when I wrote my first journal entry. I married him thinking I could fix him, and now these old behavior patterns made me truly question the covenant of my marriage. Nevertheless, I decided to put on blinders and ignored what my intuition knew as the truth.

Early on, I enjoyed everything about being married, the companionship, sharing, and building a life together. But over time, I saw my marriage going in a direction that I resisted. Because I knew that once I peeled back the layers and made my happiness a priority, it would completely disrupt everything I had grown to know for the past fifteen years.

> **07/17/2011**
>
> I keep my head down and my mouth shut, about everything!
> EVERYTHING! I open up and it goes in a different direction, then
> turns into a confrontation. I avoid it, then shut down. My life has
> been lived in shut down, total shut down mode. The tale of two
> sides; one loving — supporting; the other dictator — controlling.

In the past, whenever confronted with the truth, my husband became defensive, belligerent, and self-righteous. I felt guilty for accusing him of something he denied and decided to fake it because although I was on a path to healing from past hurts, there were still some issues I simply did not want to deal with. I became skilled at only seeing what I wanted to see; however, it was time for me to get clear in all areas of my life, no matter how messy or messed up it was. And it was a complete mess.

> **07/27/2011**
>
> I go to sleep mad, wake up mad. It is hard for me to be around him,
> like him, talk to him, afraid I will say something I can't come back
> from. No honesty. No freedom of speech without arguing. An old
> feeling keeps coming up that I can't shake. I need a distraction, but
> I had a close friend admit that she's concerned about my bourbon
> drinking. Now what outlet do I have?

As I progressed through my doctoral program, I attended a three-day residency in Atlanta. This experience heightened my excitement to be on track to earn my Doctor of Education degree. During the residency, I felt empowered in the scholarly environment where creative, critical thinking, and innovative research took place. When I returned home, I became more motivated to put every ounce of my energy into completing the program by August 2012.

I reflected on the obstacles I had faced while working on my bachelor's and master's degrees and knew that I had the ambition to finish. I genuinely enjoyed school, so I also knew the challenges that came with achieving those previous goals. History showed me that I had the drive to overcome extraordinary obstacles, but I didn't know that I still needed to face my biggest obstacle yet.

Would I have the faith, determination, and discipline required to move forward in this new dimension of learning? Could I truly get to a place of clear, honest, transparent love that I so desired and deserved? Could I learn to accept the things I simply could not change and learn to love myself?

07/28/2011

I haven't bathed in two days. I would make it three, but he returns today, so I gotta put on the face, play the role, keep my mouth shut and head down. I overslept this morning from waking up at 1 a.m. to throw some homework together. I missed the deadline by eight minutes but who cares. I don't. It's hard for me to care much about anything, so I don't. I'm hollow inside, fixed to go through the motions without regard.

I don't want anything from anybody, just left alone, completely. I've given up so much only to still be alone, empty and tired. I am so tired of feeling like this, being like this, but I struggle to be anything else. I wish I could be purged, flushed out of everything, blank and

---

then refilled with all good stuff, peace. I've tried so many times on my own only to arrive right back here. I desperately seek to keep the balance, peace, harmony that I long for, but then I have a battle with myself, my mind, my emotions. I married someone who is not capable of being sensitive to my needs the way I need it.

There is an ability to do it for everyone else but not for me. I long for something that I am never going to get. I long to be a priority. First, without a doubt. But it's gone, never realized how important it was for me to have it until adulthood. Mama and Daddy made me a priority. I was important enough to keep, raise up, and nurture. But I still need it now and I don't have it.

The closer I get to 40, the more solace I crave. I know what it's like to appear to have it all but to suffer in silence behind everything. I know what it's like to see/wish/pray for one thing and get none of it or have it come with a hefty price. I know what it's like to be empty, alone, longing to be important enough to be a priority. I know what it's like because it's Me.

The doctoral program was a different level of engagement than my previous face-to-face learning experiences. The program was intense, but the online format only added to the intensity because it required me to be entirely self-directed and focused in every way.

My habit of going to the library to study or staying up past the kid's bedtime to work on my assignments served me well. I kept all of my previous assignments from both undergraduate and graduate programs, and I intentionally focused my doctoral work to build on what I already learned. I wanted all of my formal education to be in alignment and be a bridge for future research.

I kept a reflective research journal, and that served me well because I wrote questions, ideas, and references in one place. If I learned nothing else, I knew that I had to select a research topic that I was passionate about. My passion for learning grew in new areas, and the online doctoral program served to stoke the flame that lit the way down a long, dark, and lonely tunnel. Although I was full steam ahead on this new educational journey, all work and no play made for a dull and exhausting life — a sunny get-a-way was just what this future doctor needed.

By early fall 2011, my daughter prepared for the fifth grade and my son the fourth grade. But on our way to a school function, just days before the school year started, we were hit from behind while sitting at a red light. On impact, I immediately felt pain in my neck and back. The paramedics arrived on the scene and strapped me to a gurney with a neck brace. I could not move. I had no choice but to look up. The sky was crystal clear, not one cloud, only sun.

This car accident pushed me to my breaking point. I could not ignore it any longer. God knew how to slow me down because I was on a fast track headed nowhere. I had been in a cycle of dysfunction for years; blaming others, surface thinking, impulsive and destructive thoughts, and behaviors. It was time I faced the music. I had to surrender.

As I laid on that gurney, I looked to the sky and said, "Okay, Lord, I am here. You have my full attention. I am here, and I am Yours." Fortunately, I was the only person who suffered any injuries from the accident. I was treated for neck and back pain with frequent chiropractor visits and physical therapy. As my physical body began to heal, I could not ignore the spiritual encounter I had with God in the car accident. Yet I tried to ignore it, and I continued business as usual.

08/29/2011

I cannot remember a time that I was genuinely happy, and I mean happy without the influence of alcohol or any other substance — where I was at peace that I could just melt away. I can't remember a time I felt like that or experienced it without some sort of catch or time constraint or command that felt like a gun to my head. I can't remember. It seems like stress and negativity has been my path for a while now.

My friend was right. Yet, I got mad at her truth about my drinking. I got mad at my current state and for being called out about it. I wanted a pass. A go-ahead-girl-I-understand-your-pain pass. I didn't want to take responsibility. I just wanted freedom to be and to be told that it's okay but it's not okay. Yet I struggle, daily at how to not let it be that way. A constant battle, an everlasting war. How do I get out of this? It's not working, and it hasn't worked for some time now. But yet I remain, unhappy and alone. Alone and unhappy. I'm not very good company to be around so I shut down and shut out. I can't even relax or allow myself to relax.

That damn wreck was the last thing I needed. Who has time, energy to chase a claim, file medical, go to appointments? Damn! I never envisioned 40 being or feeling like this. ...I look at some old photos of me and I don't even recognize the person in the picture. Who is she? And why does she appear to be happy when in reality it's different, so different that it doesn't have a word. So strange that

> it's hard to describe so opposite of what everybody sees, thinks, believes that it's unknown. Mystery.
>
> The more I try the harder it gets to overcome. Pretty soon I will just stop trying. I'm worn out from all the trying – all the giving – all to everybody but me. I'm so sick of being on the back burner. So sick of, "wait till I finish and then ", so sick of chasing happiness.

I taught multiple online college courses as an adjunct professor, in addition to my full-time status as a doctoral student. I gained experience in higher education on many levels, but it was still not a substitute for the loneliness I felt at home. I also continued to fight a daily battle with depression. I found myself not only drinking socially but also privately —to numb all of my pain.

The closer it got to my birthday, the more reflective I became, and I wrote down my feelings, which was my usual pattern.

> 09/21/2011
>
> In exactly one week, (Lord willing) I will turn 40! 4-0, Wow! I want to do a documentary. I wish I had already done one, but maybe these journals will help put things together one day. I don't know if I ever imagined what 40 looked like or felt like. At 20, viewing 40 had to be like looking at the end of the world, still here I am and it doesn't feel like the end, but rather the beginning of something wonderful... I want this new chapter to be about laughter, hard and often, even if the only one laughing is me. I want my joy back.
>
> Every day is a blessing. Every day is a gift! I want my kids to know me. I want them to know how much I love them and how much they

mean to me. I want them to know I appreciate the opportunity to be their mother even when I'm overwhelmed and not always nice. I want them to know that they each saved my life and gave me a reason to move forward. I want them to know that I have feelings, I get scared and that I cry (sometimes a lot), but that I know where my strength comes from and that God is my keeper!

In late 2011, my husband and I took a trip. For quite some time, I felt like although I was married, I was a single parent, so I welcomed the opportunity to rekindle my relationship with the man I married. But the trip was not the one-on-one, romantic getaway that I desperately desired. Instead, it was a trip with a group of people — most of whom he worked with — and every activity was done as a group.

I expected the trip to renew the love and deep affection that once existed in my marriage, but that was not the case. The only thing that changed was the warm weather and beautiful location. We still treated each other with a cavalier casualness that bordered on disrespect. We did not honor each other in private or among the group. Instead, we cut each other off in mid-sentence, used the other as the focal point for an offhand joke that was demeaning in an effort to get a laugh from other people, spoke about the other person with low-level sarcasm that slowly gnawed at the bones of our relationship. This was our marriage. This was our pattern.

But one day, while out with the group, I learned the hard way that tequila is much more potent in places outside of the United States than what I was used to. As a result, I spent the night passed out in my bed, and the next day I woke up with a massive headache, alone, on a wet mattress. He was extremely upset with me, and as a result, I spent a lot of time alone after that night.

> **11/16/2011**
>
> It has pretty much been a solo kind of day. Just me doing my own thing. So, I sit alone watching and waiting for the sun to set. Lord thank you for the solitude which I treasure, but company is good every now and then, stimulating conversation, like-minded people, critical thinkers, but who are they and where are they? A lone intellect in a busy, numb, world too overly stimulated with everything and everybody else.

Needless to say, this trip forced me to grow and grow some more. But this trip also provided the rejuvenation I needed to focus on my doctoral studies. The tropical environment gave me space to think long and hard about my current situation. I returned with my skin darker and my mind wiser. It was time to own my truth.

CHAPTER 13

Good Counsel

> "And here you yourself must be an example to them of good deeds of every kind. Let everything you do reflect your love of the truth and the fact that you are in dead earnest about it." *-Titus 2:7*

O VER THE YEARS, I conditioned myself to ignore the patterns of dysfunction in my marriage. The way we communicated was by *not* communicating. The silent treatment lasted longer and longer, weeks went by, and we barely spoke a word to each other, yet we were the life of the party in public. When we lived in Wisconsin, I chose to focus on my children and school, and although my truth could no longer be ignored, I was still afraid to rock the boat. Nevertheless, I had to step out of the boat and keep my eyes on Jesus.

I was afraid, yet I was filled with joy because he was with me, and I had to trust Him and move in faith. I had to make a change. I had to be strong, be courageous, and do the messy work to finally get to a place of peace, harmony, and happiness I so desired and deserved.

Early 2012 came, and the news of Whitney Houston's death in February, followed by Trayvon Martin's killing in March, only complicated my feelings about life and what was happening in the Black community. I was hurt and felt deeply about the loss of both of these members of society. My heart went out to Trayvon's mother, especially since I was a mother of a Black son.

> **03/20/2012**
> Skittles. Iced Tea. Cell Phone. Skittles. Iced Tea. Cell Phone. Lord, protect my children. Lord protect my son. This is a common plea from every Black mother, I'm sure... Trayvon was sent to his father's house and simply took a walk to the store for a snack. Bang! Did he get to eat the skittles? Was the iced tea the cool drink he couldn't wait to enjoy as he walked to the gated community where his dad stayed? His last phone call was to his friend, a girl. Lord help us all. Lord, protect my children. Skittles. Iced Tea. Cell Phone.

April 2012 marked ten years that Mama went to heaven to be with the Lord. I decided that I would honor her by planting a tree in our backyard. However, my decision did not come without justification, opposition, and justification as to what tree to plant and where to plant it. A simple task turned into a big argument.

> **04/12/2012**
> It's hard to describe how I'm feeling right now. We had an argument this morning about a tree and digging a hole in the yard. The

other day, we had a spirited discussion about the thawing of the pork chops. Both were minimal but I am really angry at his lack of sensitivity to my needs and how significant this week is for me.

I'm mad because it brings up old feelings of how he wasn't there for me the way I needed him to be back then. I'm mad because from the outside all looks fine — but it's not. I'm not fine and don't know when I have been fine. I live under a constant mask, but the drinking only creates more damage and it's not worth it. Yet I have no other constant support, it's all temporary. It seems like the closer I get to my dissertation the less enthusiastic I become to even finish. Where is the golden ticket? Where's the pay off? I'm literally going out of my mind and at what cost?

My soul support system, my soul motivation went to heaven ten years ago. I didn't know what to do then and don't know what to do now. Over the years I have tried and clung to several things all in an effort to mask the deep pain, hurt and loneliness that I really feel. Nothing has been able to fill the void or comfort of my aching loneliness. Every day I try to keep my head up. I am more isolated now than I ever was... Starved. Shut out. Shut down. Alone. Lonely... even with people around, always lonely. Peace, joy, happiness, harmony, this is all I want — all I ever wanted. I just want to live in peace.

04/13/2012
I dreamt that Allison and I were looking for dorm rooms. Each door opened showed a different colored room with different size beds. We finally settled on a room with one twin bed and one sleeper sofa with a full-size bed. We were happy roommates, laughing. We

> made it work. Next, I had a dream that me and the kids were at the house on Clay Street, making breakfast. Mama was there too. We were all smiling. Bacon smell filled the air. Mama was the picture of health and happiness. We sat at the dining room table. I didn't want to wake up. I didn't want to leave. It felt good to be home!

Meanwhile, summer 2012 was a season of profound transition on many levels. First, my beloved dog died. Second, I lost a good friend to suicide. Next, I began to write my doctoral dissertation. Then, I filed for divorce.

> **06/11/2012**
> Everybody plays a fool and this is exactly what I have been played for the past 18 years. "Wow" is all I can really get out. But what I uncovered gives confirmation for what I already suspected but damn, really? Why and how have I deserved this? Sigh... I'm all out of tears. I'm just ready to move forward. I want to be an adult about it but the juvenile in me wants to go completely off. I mean buck-f'ing wild... but I gotta keep my priorities straight. I gotta keep my kids safe and on solid ground, even if I'm falling apart. But just like everything else God's got it and HE got me too and HE got the kids. HE also got my husband who needs help. This is beyond me. All I know is that I am finished!

I've always been told not to go looking for something unless you are ready to deal with what you might find. That day in June became the day I was prepared to confront what I found. And what I found was the truth in black and white.

I found the truth about my marriage and lack of commitment to me. I found a series of direct messages to various people that spanned the life of my relationship with my husband. And the tone and temperament in those direct messages told me everything that I suspected but chose not to believe. I was not the only woman in my husband's life.

As a matter of fact, there were more women than I ever cared to know about, but I could no longer hide my head in the sand or wear the rose-colored glasses anymore. It was time to get a clear vision of my situation and my future.

06/12/2012

I still feel sick to my stomach. I've barely eaten today. The sight, thought, sound of him makes me ill. "Wow" is all I keep coming back to. But I've got to tackle this just like everything else, on my own: make a plan, keep focused, stay determined until it is done. Lord, please keep my children safe. Sleep won't come...my mind will not rest. This is the last thing I need right now, yet I know there is no mistake with God's timing. I will trust in the Lord with all of my heart and lean not unto my own understanding. I do not understand what is happening or what the outcome will be, but I am trusting the Lord to see me through this just like HE has seen me through everything else.

06/13/2012

I had every intention to visit the cemetery this morning, but the gate was locked. I wanted to go there to mourn the slow and painful death that I am experiencing right now. This hurts more than I know how to express. And all I keep asking is why? What have I done to deserve this? But I am trusting in the Lord with all of my heart and leaning not unto my own understanding. None of this makes sense. None. It's hard to believe that someone so well respected and held in such high regard, in public, could be capable of something like this.

But unfortunately, I know first-hand that it is true, and the truth is killing me right now, but in a small way it is also setting me free. It is also making me stronger. But in this very moment, I feel helpless and weak. But my strength is made perfect in weakness.

When I filed for divorce, it was a shock to most people because the public perception of my marriage appeared fully intact. But to me, it was only a matter of time because, behind the scenes, things were not all that good.

Oh yes, we had some good times during our decade-plus of marriage. We became good at appearing good. But for years, I accepted raggedy behavior in place of love, respect, honesty, and friendship. The warning signs were there prior to our getting married, but I had decided to ignore them because I was the chosen one. Keep in mind, he was older and had traveled the world before we ever met, yet he chose little ol' me from Kentucky to be his wife. I was the chosen one. I could make this work. Right? Nope. When I faced my truth and learned that the dysfunction and denial in my marriage ran deeper than I could fix, I knew I had to make a choice: save my marriage or save me.

I chose me.

At first, I thought the gut-wrenching reality of my marriage was punishment for all the horrible things I did in my past, but I came to realize that God does not specialize in revenge. God is a God of mercy who specializes in love, hope, and renewal. However, nothing about my decision to file for divorce came easy. I had to fight for my freedom. I had to deal with me. I had to learn to make myself a priority and discover who I was, so each day, I took a bold step to self-love, self-care, and self-knowing.

I made appointments and saw an attorney, a pastor, a doctor, and a therapist, all in the same week. I slowly dialed back my alcohol consumption and took in more water because I needed clarity. Then, I refocused my energy on prayer and meditation; I reignited my habit of writing Scripture on notecards and placing those cards in places where I saw them on a regular basis. At a therapy session, my new therapist believed that I had formed a dysfunctional pattern of behavior and conditioned myself to ignore what I knew was the truth, like the huge red flag I ignored when my wedding gown was ruined on the flight to Hawaii just days before the ceremony. I chose to ignore *all* the red flags because I was in love with what I *thought* was love.

All of my relationships before marriage were dysfunctional, abusive, and filled with denial. I did not value myself, so how could I expect anyone else to value me? This included the man I decided to marry. Howver, my marriage was never physically abusive, so any sign of abuse, deception, manipulation, control, or neglect, I dismissed because at least I wasn't getting punched in the stomach or being dragged across the floor, as was the case in some of my previous relationships. I rationalized any janky behavior in my marriage by reflecting on the physical abuse I endured in the past, and decided to fake it until I made it.

I also connected this same dysfunctional pattern of behavior when it came to dealing with my family; I had become skilled at grinning and nodding in compliance to anything that went on around me to publicly appear like all was okay — when in reality, it wasn't. This reflection helped me put that feeling into perspective.

05/21/2012

Forced bonding. I can't pick my family, but I can choose to keep them at a distance and establish some boundaries — walls going up. Something I don't think I've ever done. I've been vulnerable the first forty years of my life, but I refuse to be vulnerable and naive the next forty. I know better. So now I need to do better at making choices. I have the freedom to choose — without regret.

I have been hurt by those closest to me. Forgiveness has allowed me to move forward, but I'm still healing and operating out of a place of wisdom that I realize everybody is not at, nor do they understand. But I have to be true to my freedom to choose and step up when it results in consequences that need to be dealt with. I'm tired of stuff being forced on me or quilted into something — including relationships with my family... I desire authentic meaningful relationships that generate positive support without manipulation, jealousy, resentment or animosity. I've decided not to have that in my life. It is what it is and that's just the way it is.

I'm tired of always being the initiator or the enabler. The choice is mine. I have the freedom to choose.

I wrote more consistently during this time because writing in my journal was everything, and it allowed me to get creative in a space that was mine and mine only.

06/15/2012

I'm gonna push through this / I just have to / I gotta do this for ME / Cause I sho n hell ain't doing it for you / Who are you? / I don't even know anymore / don't think I ever did / It scares me to know that your true colors were hid / Before – I did not want to see, but I do now / and you can't deny / But then again you will try / Like you always do / I'm not worried because the data is true / So now the consequences come and it won't be easy / But I'm rejoicing at the thought of being free and breezy / Although not totally.... we made two beautiful lives together and they are innocent / but none of us became your priority / time & time again you took authority / and made decisions / that will change all of our lives, but time will make way for new beginnings / And as I push on, I'm gonna keep on living / Giving God all the glory because I have plenty of reasons to / And even if I may still cry, sometimes / I'm moving forward without you!

A week after I had decided to pursue a divorce, my doctoral committee was confirmed. The first requirement was to schedule a mandatory conference call with the committee's chairperson for introductions and to share ideas of possible research studies and methodology to complete the study. I set a date and time for the call, praying that I would make it through without a complete mental breakdown at this very crucial point of my doctoral program.

Once we were on the phone, I let my chairperson lead the conversation. I took notes, and at some point, I put my pen down and started to pace the floor as I listened to him talk. My heart raced as I heard all the demands a doctoral study required; this was some next-level commitment and focus, and I was thoroughly outside of my comfort zone. I held my breath and tried to fight back the tears. When he asked me if I had any questions, I exhaled, cleared my throat, and told him that I had to share something very personal. I explained how the recent events in my personal life would directly affect my ability to meet the demands he just shared. As I spoke, I had a complete breakdown on the phone. While I told him of my impending divorce and need to find a new place to live, the other end of the phone was stone silent.

Then, after I had finished sobbing and slobbering, the committee chairperson responded in a calm and collected voice, giving me the option to withdraw from the program to focus on my personal family matters and ensuring that I could re-enter the program once things settled down. I inhaled, exhaled, and made my voice just as calm and collected as his before responding, "Absolutely not," and expressing that it was not optional for me to withdraw from the program; I was too close to my goal and needed this doctoral degree now more than ever. He agreed with my decision, and together, we designed a plan for me to complete my literature review, which included a provision that I would submit bi-weekly progress reports so that I would remain accountable.

But even with this plan in place, there were weeks when I stayed on track with my progress to get things done, and then there were weeks when I struggled. Nevertheless, I attempted to remain on track by taking it one day at a time — one scholarly article at a time.

06/22/2012

The truth can rip you apart. It can feel like being kicked in the stomach and punched in the face all at the same time. Heart racing, adrenaline pumping, breathing so fast that you feel like you are going to choke. I try to steady myself, but the trembling doesn't stop. I ache. I'm numb. I'm hollow, completely empty... I need a time out. I welcome the thought of one. My logical mind goes into the planning phase, while the radical mind says just go, do it, NOW!

I have been conditioned to be in a box and now I'm trying to train myself to get out of the box in order to get to the essence of who I really am. I want my joy back. At my last therapy session, I was asked what I would most like to be doing, if there were no boundaries. I broke down. The tears streamed and I had a hard time pulling myself together. When I finally got myself together to think about what I wanted most, I came up with this list:

- I want to write.
- I want to be published both professionally and personally.
- I want to speak.
- I want to travel.
- I want to encourage, empower and share my experiences in order to help someone else.
- I want my life to be used as a living testimony to the goodness of God and all that He has done for me.
- I want to be healed, so that I may help others in their healing.
- I am hurting right now, body rocked with pain. Lord, help me to heal.

In between all the pain, I never stopped praying. I prayed for my family with special prayers for my husband. I prayed for my friends and my enemies. I prayed for patience as I journeyed through this extremely painful process. I prayed for sanity because on every level, I completely lost my mind.

06/23/2012

It's harder to get out of the bed on the weekends because the kids don't have to be anywhere. It took everything in me to put my feet on the ground and stand up this morning, because once I did then it would start all over again — the pain, the tears, THE PAIN! But I did. I got up and I forced myself to ride my bike instead of my run/walk combo. Next, I washed and cleaned out the van. And as I cleaned, I envisioned us / me living in my van and you know what, once it was cleaned out it didn't look half bad. The van is paid for, so I wouldn't have to struggle to pay rent. Oh, who am I kidding? Where am I going to go? How is this going to ever work? Lord, keep me, help me and bless me...give me favor in this mess.

Later this same day....

I just got off the phone with my chairperson. I informed him of what was going on in my personal life because as another professional in my circle he needs to know. He supports my decision — whatever it is, and whatever I want. And he wants to see me through this program — to completion. I couldn't talk to him about any of it without crying. When will I ever stop crying?

I was scared, but I had to dig beyond any place that was familiar to find new courage to file for divorce and move forward. I made the decision to move out of the five-bedroom house we had purchased in a predominately white suburban neighborhood just a few years earlier, but I did not know where I would go. This presented a whole new set of challenges because here I was, a soon-to-be-divorced, Black female with two children, looking for a place to live in a rural area with a history of invisible lines that separated Black from white housing. Yet I just knew I could not remain in a house, no matter how lovely that was not a home or a marriage that was broken beyond repair.

I decided to use all of my energy to repair myself so that I could be strong for my children and be strong enough to complete my doctoral degree. In the midst of all of this, I had another mental and physical breakdown — as I had finally gained a healthy amount of weight from the weight loss a few years earlier, the pounds once again evaporated because I could not eat. Water became my drink of choice so that I wouldn't get dehydrated.

After I saw the rock-gut truth, the reality of everything made me sick, and I could not keep any food down, but I still had to take responsibility for letting things get so messy. I cried all day, and then I cried myself to sleep at night. The children thought I was grieving over the loss of our dog, and part of me was, but I also grieved for the death of my marriage. I grieved for the death of the person I once was. I went inside myself to try and sort things out and got clear on my plan. I only shared details of my personal life with a select few, so I appeared okay in public. But the only noticeable thing was my drastic weight loss. In the meantime, I poured myself into my journals and to my therapist.

06/30/2012

My therapist is filled with so much wisdom. Her perspective on things is very eye opening and has caused me to further pause, consider and reflect. Especially her view on the early years, the very beginning, how it all came to be for me, from her view. I was open to receive her perspective, much more open to the truth than I've ever been. Clarity. It hit me during my run this morning. I cried. I had to stop, catch my breath and cry some more. I had to acknowledge the truth. I have to walk in truth.

From my therapist's perspective, somewhere Daddy Boots messed up with his daughter (my grandmother Ann). He then saw the mistake repeated and passed down to his granddaughter (my biological mother Cookie). The knowledge did not get passed. The capacity was not there. Maybe the hope and chance and prayer were there for things to turn out different especially when my biological mother, Cookie and biological father, James were together. But once they split up, then reality took over with the only chance for something different was to save the great-granddaughter (me) and give me a chance to do things different, give me stability, security, love, attention, affection.

Give me a home. Give me a future. Give me a chance. Thank you, God for my chance!

My therapy sessions continued to be painful. I cried. I balled up in a fetal position on the floor. I fell apart. I had some deep self-examination ahead of me and what I uncovered was a complete mess.

But that mess was all me. It was my life, and I had to face the old me in order to create a new me, a new life. And that's what I desired more than anything, a new me. I also wanted a completed and an approved dissertation so I could be finished with school once and for all.

CHAPTER 14

Good Run

I STRUGGLED A LOT, BUT eventually accepted the fact that my marriage was over. I also accepted the truth that my life would be forever changed. Divorce sucks, simple and plain. And even with the pain of the divorce, as my mind was in complete shambles, I still needed to meet the demands of my doctoral dissertation committee, parent my two children, *and* somehow find the energy to work.

By this time, I only worked as an adjunct professor teaching online college classes. This part-time position provided me the flexibility I needed to focus on family and school while designing the new life I deserved. However, my mind was in heavy transformation. Some days I would get through it. Other days I desired a straitjacket and a tranquilizer.

07/18/2012

Lord, give my mind rest so that I may have a good night's sleep free from worry or negative thoughts and bad dreams. Lord help my mind to be stayed on You — all the time! I feel like I am one step away from slipping into a very deep and long depression. I am empty with no more to give to no one. I feel as if I don't know how to do anything anymore. My tank is on "E". I just want peace, rest, renewal and happiness. I want and desire a life of happiness. *God grant me the serenity to accept the things I cannot change, courage to change the things I can, and wisdom to know the difference.*

Each morning during this time, I dropped the kids off at a summer day camp and went for a walk in the local park. I used this time to walk and talk to God, desperately seeking His guidance to carry me through this process. Most times, I cried more than I walked, and other times I couldn't even talk. But one morning, I decided to take my walk to the next level, and I ran to the blue trashcan on the trail. I formed a habit of running and gradually increased my distance by setting small goals. I ran to the blue trashcan.

Next, I ran to the park bench, then the light pole. I repeated this routine until I ran one mile without stopping. The more I ran, the more I began to feel better about my future. I began to feel better about myself. Fresh air and movement helped clear some of the clutter in my mind, which helped me get clear on what I needed in my life.

I prayed a lot . . . *about everything*. I would kneel to pray and then shift into a plank to pray "The Lord's Prayer" — holding the position until I said, "Amen!" With each prayer-plank exercise, I felt my core get stronger. God moved in my life in a big way at that time, and I became hopeful for the bright future ahead. While my body was in motion, my mind was still. During one of my runs, I had a talk with God that went like this...

07/20/2012

Me: My life has been ripped apart.

God: But where it has been ripped, it can be put back together again, even better.

Me: I feel hollow — a shell of what I once was.

God: But what you used to be was no good. Time for a new you.

Me: But I don't even know what a new me is...

God: You don't have to know. I do. And it will all be revealed in due time.

Me: Lord, help me to keep going to keep moving forward.

God: I will. Keep quiet. Be still. I got this. You are my child and I will take care of you.

My routine became, drop off kids, run in the park, go to the public library to work on the dissertation, pick up kids from school, spend quality time with them, feed and put them to bed, work on the dissertation, fall to sleep with the light on and an article on my chest, repeat. I still wasn't able to eat during this time because stress and anxiety lived in my gut, and I couldn't keep any food down, so I started to drink protein shakes to supplement. I also attended strength-training classes at the Family Activity Center.

My mind and body started to take on a new shape. Running and strength training helped to transform my pain into power.

In August 2012, my therapist started me on medication to help manage my anxiety and depression. I just wanted to be okay, even though I did not know what okay would look like. I reached out to Dr. Robinson, and nothing I told her was a surprise.

Her response after I announced that I was getting a divorce was, "I've been praying for this. You need a real-life! Your mind and body need freedom, and I knew when you were my student that you were under a lot of pressure, more pressure than you wanted anybody to know about. But you are ready for this, and you can handle it now. You have power now. It doesn't feel good going through, and every knock is a boost to get you stronger. You are strong. You are special. You are anointed. You have the ability to process, and that's a blessing."

I started all over emotionally, spiritually, physically, and financially. I worked multiple part-time (adjunct) positions, but my past income streams were cut in half. I had decided to resign from my full-time position before all hell broke loose in my life, and I filed for divorce; therefore, the security of full-time income and medical benefits were gone. My adjunct teaching positions relied heavily on university budgeting and student enrollment; therefore, I did not know from one semester to the next if I would be asked to teach an online course. My primary income sources were my student loan refund, tax refund, and whatever frugal choice I made with my spending.

Running became a freeway for me to stay active with fresh air and exercise. It became another form of therapy. I read running magazines and learned the importance of nutrition along with strength training for running endurance.

On the first Saturday of every month, the local extension office sponsored a morning walk. The reward for meeting and walking at 8:30 a.m. one Saturday a month, an all-access pass to the Family Activity Center. This center offered fitness classes. The first Saturday of every month, I roused my sleepy children out of their beds, and we all went for a walk. This allowed me to get not one but three all-access passes to the Family Activity Center. I had no money, so this was how I attended a strength training class several times a month. Over time, I improved my mental fitness and my physical fitness. I also made healthier choices when I shopped for groceries. And I slowly began to take in more fruits and vegetables and became stronger and stronger every day.

08/13/2012

It's a hard realization when you understand what you never had, but then you know it and it kind of blows your mind — like "Wow, I never knew it could be like this" or "What? You mean all I had to do was ask and make it a requirement, then I would get it??" or "Now, you know what I require and I still don't get it, but it's not for my lack of asking, it is for your lack of knowledge and true understanding of what it means, what I want and how to give it to me."

Today I gave voice to this realization. I have finally come to understand his true inability to give me what I NEED and to love, nurture, protect and take care of me the EXACT way I need to be loved, nurtured, protected and taken care of. He wants me to go back to the person I was when we first met. I am not the same person I was eighteen years ago.

My requirements are so much different now. I am trying to understand what I want as a soon-to-be 41-year-old woman. I am trying
to understand how to simply take care of me and to love myself
— what it really takes to love me. I'm trying to learn to give myself
oxygen in order for me to stay alive so I can help someone else.

All this time it has been the total opposite which explains why I have
been fighting for air for the past 40 years... just trying to catch my
breath long enough to go and save the next person and the next...
Well, now I am in the fight to simply save myself and all that comes
with it. I am in survival mode now — but I look forward to thriving
and being the best "me" there is and truly loving, embracing and
listening to that intelligent, wise, independent, strong, determined,
bold woman that I know is there. Each day, she reveals herself to
me in the most profound ways. She really showed up and showed
out today and I am glad. Thank you. Thank you!

At one point, I thought I could remain in the marriage and the
house we shared until the kids finished the school year. Then I
tried to rationalize that I would stay until the winter break. None
of those ideas worked, so at the end of August, a week after the
school year started, we sat around the kitchen table and informed
the children that we were getting a divorce — more like I broke
the news to them. Beforehand, my husband and I had agreed that
we would tell the children together, but when the time came, the
spotlight was put directly on me with the statement, "Sit down,
your mother has something to tell you."

And with this, I looked my two children in their sweet faces
and announced that I planned to divorce their dad and move out.

I did the best I could without breaking into tears, but my son's tears were immediate, yet my daughter sat quiet, with no emotion on her face. She was my ten-year-old intuitive, strong-willed, sweet child, very observant, and something told me that she saw this announcement coming.

On the other hand, my sensitive, big-hearted, empathetic son had plenty of questions, and he cried a long time before he could get all of his questions out. In his eight-year-old mind, my son thought I did not love him anymore and that when I moved, he would never see me again. I assured him that I loved him and that I was still his mother, no matter where I lived, and that although things would be different when I moved, he would still see me and be with me. Next, he wanted to know if I was still getting him a birthday present since he would turn nine in a few weeks. I said yes, and a smile washed over his face as he wiped his tears away.

My very mature adolescent daughter then asked her one *and only* question: she wanted to know if she would have to ride a new school bus. I told her that the routine would be different, but she would remain on the same school bus and attend the same school. And with this answer, she appeared to be somewhat satisfied. Finally, my husband spoke up and announced that he would take the kids out for a slushy, so the three of them left the house . . . and I went upstairs to pray and plank.

09/03/2012

I do not want to be married anymore. There! I said it. I have been saying it to myself and now I am saying it out loud. Today, I said it directly to him since nothing else I've been saying has been heard. I had to speak up and make it clear. I have to get rid of the old to make way for the new — standing on my own and being fully committed to God without distraction or fear, without regret, but moving forward on Faith.

I want more out of my life and I want to position myself to receive more. I want all that God has in store for me and I want to be a light to help others who have found themselves in a dark situation.

I want to guide them through the transformation of turning their pain into power and to be courageous enough to stand up, stand out and run to their victory.

CHAPTER 15

Good Transformation

> "But the good man walks along in the ever-brightening light
> of God's favor; the dawn gives way to morning splendor."
> – Proverbs 3:18

WITH THE NEWS OF the divorce out to the children, I also let those in my circle know about my decision to move out and move on with my life, even if I had no clue what that looked like. Fortunately, around this time, a good friend was scheduled to attend a conference in San Francisco and thought it would be a good idea if I tagged along for a change of pace. It had been a while since I traveled, and I jumped at the chance to see the West Coast. It was the first time I could take a trip with just me, for me. I purchased my ticket without hesitation. On the flight to California, I wrote in my journal.

09/04/2012

My life is on such a different path than what it was fifteen years ago. It's hard to describe. For the first time in my life I am putting on my oxygen mask first. I am on a mission to save myself, to love myself, to take care of myself — all through the will and the power of God. I want to be in direct position for HIM to be first in my life, for HIM to take control of my life, for HIM to direct my life! Up in the air, the sky is blue, the clouds are puffy and white. The conditions are bright, sunny, full of promise, hope — light.

This is the feeling that I want, a feeling of promise. A feeling of hope. I also want this for my children because I know that God wants it for me and for them. I don't want to be distracted by nonsense. I want to rise above the clouds — fly past the grayness and get to my clear blue, bright puffiness. The future that God has for me is so bright, I can't look directly at it for too long, blinded by the light. I have to take it in small doses, but Lord I'm ready. Give me what YOU know I can handle. Keep me on the right path. Show me the way.

The second day in San Francisco, while my friend attended the conference, I volunteered and served breakfast to the homeless at Glide Memorial Church. It was a humbling experience and one that left an impression on me. There are a lot of people in the world who are in need. The day before departing San Francisco, I took a walk across the Golden Gate Bridge. Walking across the bridge affirmed that I had what it took to make it on my own, and as I walked, I prayed for the Lord to give me the strength I needed to move forward.

I returned home and felt renewed, but it didn't take long before I felt like I was slipping back with doubt and fear. This fear and anxiety gave way to a spike in my blood pressure, and at a visit to my medical doctor, she said, "Given all that you have been through in such a short time, you have made great improvement. You are so strong. Never doubt how strong you are."

I double up on my therapy sessions, and it was during this intensity that I had a complete breakdown . . . and breakthrough. At one of the visits, the therapist kept pushing me to get to the core of why I am so guarded, why I won't be vulnerable and trust myself, and why I won't be vulnerable with Cookie? Why do I keep waiting for the other shoe to drop and not trust? I kept dancing around the issue and found other things to blame it on, but the therapist kept pushing (she's good!). And finally, it came out. I could not be vulnerable and trust because of my family's past hurt and betrayal towards me when Mama died. That type of hurt damaged my core, and although it had been ten years, that is the source of my walls that I would not let come down.

At this truth, I broke into uncontrollable tears. Every milestone that I had accomplished in the past decade, I longed for Mama in a way that I could not find words, and without the full, sincere support of family, I felt lost and alone, even having gained so much. Now here I was, stepping out on my own and establishing my independence in a way Mama always believed I could. When Mama gave me her blessing and sent me out into the world, she knew in her heart that I would someday return *home*. And when I reflected on what she said to me before I moved to Hawaii and got married, her words were, "This is your chance to go and see the world. Go and see it 'cause I have already lived my life and seen all that I'm going to see."

Mama never said anything about being happy in my marriage or living a good life with my husband; she simply said go and see the world. So, once she gave me her wisdom, she knew I would one day gain my own wisdom to do what was best for me. And now that time had come. At the end of September 2012, I turned forty-one, I signed a one-year lease and picked up the keys to my new place.

09/30/2012

Today has been very painful. Literally so much pain that I broke-down crying in front of everybody. I have pain in the left backside of my neck, shoulder pain that is paralyzing. For the second time in about a year I was forced on my back unable to move, nothing to do but look up. I was forced to look up. But this pain is different. A different cycle of pain. A different reaction a different outcome. I broke down in sobbing heaves, tears rolling down my face, trying to catch my breath; crying and I couldn't stop it. It came from the pit of my stomach. My kids and my husband stood, stunned, watching my breakdown. The pain came out of nowhere. I've slept on the futon upstairs for the past few months, but I shouldn't have neck and back pain hurt this bad.

I imagine the symbol behind the pain and the timing is the resur-facing of grief. The grief due to the loss, the END of a chapter. But the breakdown makes way for a breakthrough to something new, something different – a different cycle. Lord, I lay all my aches, pains, worry and tears at the altar. I trust and believe that YOU got this and that YOUR will, will prevail. I pray for peace, harmony and smoothness in the transition, in the move, in the cycle.

> I pray for protection of my children and for YOU to do what YOU do in their father's life. Thank you for this day. Thank you for this moment. I love YOU!

Early October, I moved out of the house I purchased with my husband and rented a small remodeled house on the other side of town. My new residence was just a few blocks away from Henry Clay Street, the street where I grew up. For the first time, I found myself entirely on my own — I had my own place. That first night, I made a pallet on the upstairs bedroom floor so that I would have somewhere to sleep. I had no bedroom furniture.

My new residence was located next to the railroad tracks. I laid there looking up at the ceiling and letting the sound of the train lull me to sleep. The following morning, I awoke rested, peaceful, and grateful. When I went downstairs, I felt good about my decision and the transformation I was in. The sun beamed through the newly replaced windows and reflected off the hardwood floors. I was on the right track to a better life. I moved at my own pace, took my time about everything, and allowed God to direct my path.

That night I fixed my first meal in my new place: grilled chicken, roasted Brussel sprouts, and a baked sweet potato with a half glass of wine. I sat on the one bar stool I had purchased from Goodwill and ate at the kitchen counter. As I ate, I looked around in amazement that I was finally on my own. I also couldn't believe how good the Brussel sprouts tasted. It was the first time I ever eaten any — and the first time I could do so without explaining "why" to anyone.

When the children stayed overnight at my new place, I did not have a television, so the three of us played Uno for entertainment and cuddled up and told stories until we fell asleep on the floor.

Additionally, I traded in the mini-van and purchased a car that I liked. Slowly, I acquired furniture.

Meanwhile, the grueling divorce mediation resulted in joint custody, and I adjusted to a parenting schedule. The most difficult part of the divorce was not being present with my children daily. Since day one, it had always been the three of us, together full-time. I cried myself to sleep every night they spent at their dad's house and slept with the lights on when I was home by myself. However, although I was lonely without the kids, I wasn't alone.

I knew God was with me.

10/31/2012

Peace that surpasses understanding. This is how I feel when I wake up in the mornings. I look at my surroundings and I feel peace. Thank you, God, for YOUR grace and protection that covers me through the night. Thank YOU for YOUR watchful angels that sit and watch to make sure no harm comes to me or my children or the safe place YOU have provided for us to dwell. Thank YOU for mercy which is new every morning. Thank YOU for kindness and continue to give me wisdom in all things. Be in my mouth, my tone and my attitude. Help me in my parenting. I love you God, have YOUR way and take control of this situation.

Therefore, I set a study schedule and kept myself accountable for the list of goals my doctoral chairperson expected of me every other week. It was difficult to focus, but I set small goals and took long naps when I simply could not read or write another word. My mind was in heavy transformation.

Although I missed my children when they were away from me, I improved my attitude about the situation and used it to my advantage. The greatest gift I could give to my children and myself was to finish school — one final time. So, on the weekends they spent at their dad's house, I spent at the law library of a nearby campus working on my dissertation. I packed a lunch, coffee, and water and prioritized being at the library as soon as the doors opened. The library atmosphere always allowed me to be laser-focused on my studies with minimal distractions. And, for the first time in my adult life, I made my spiritual and physical well-being a priority with prayer, water, fresh air, and exercise. This practice gave me a life of peace and contentment. I felt hopeful even as I cried. I scheduled regular meetings with my doctoral committee chairperson to be kept accountable. I wanted to be finished with school once and for all.

My research went through various stages and was resubmitted for Institutional Review Board approval more than once. I had chosen a qualitative case study as my research method because of my love for writing; what I hoped would come easy for me to complete proved to be anything but. There were many times I simply wanted to say, "Fuck it, I can't do this." However, a force beyond my control kept pressing me forward. I could not give up. I had to persist.

I printed off articles and carried them with me no matter where I went. If I was in the doctor's office, I read and annotated an article. If I was in the car rider line to pick the kids up from school, I read and annotated an article. I read articles before I went to sleep. I read articles as I waited for the laundry to dry. I designed a system with colored tabs to keep my information organized and purchased binders and clear file boxes. When my mind became too cloudy with information or exhausted from all the nuances of the divorce,

I laced up my shoes and went for a walk. I felt hopeful as I walked. I felt like I could overcome any obstacle, and I did.

In the midst of everything, I formed a new habit of daily walk/talk/run with God. I accepted more part-time teaching assignments and became a master at managing my time to meet various deadlines.

08/12/2013

Although the divorce is not officially over yet, this past year has been filled with lessons, triumphs and LOVE! It took a crisis to really expose what I was made of. It also exposed the true character of those in my circle, just as Dr. Robinson predicted. God has changed my circle. I have learned to accept where some relationships are, at this point. I had to give my energy and time to what truly brought me peace, joy and overall happiness.

I learned to be true to the things that were a positive influence in my life and rid myself of all things negative (this included people). I learned to live life on my own terms, and this has not been an easy task but my heart desired it so I've learned to trust God to do the rest. I was awestruck at what God had done in such a short time. But deep down I knew that God specialized in doing the impossible.

I never dreamed of living on my own surrounded by peace but this is what I so deeply desired and God showed up in a big way.

My divorce was finalized in late fall 2013. That same year in November, I completed my first 5k race. This accomplishment gave me the confidence to register and complete several other races, which included a half-marathon that would take place in April 2014.

The night before I ran my first half-marathon, I found a Scripture to encourage myself, wrote it on a slip of paper, and placed the paper inside the bottom of my shoe. As I ran the 13.1 miles, there were times I felt weary. I was exhausted, but when I felt like I couldn't take another step, I recalled the Scripture and began to say it out loud like a cadence — each step infusing me with renewed energy, and soon, I felt my inner strength grow. Each step sent a direct message to the devil that he would not defeat me. I had the victory.

As I ran, I forgot about my pain and remembered the goodness of God and all He had done for me. I remembered my friend Allison. I remembered all the hell I had gone through when Mama passed away and how I survived. I remembered giving birth to my daughter, struggling with motherhood, and how I survived. I remembered giving birth to my son, enduring additional surgery to remove a tumor on my left ovary, and how I survived.

I remembered Clay Street, I remembered Texas, I remembered Hawaii, I remembered Washington D.C., and I remembered Wisconsin. I remembered school and how I survived. I survived divorce. I survived being abandoned by my mother. I survived. I survived it all.

After I crossed the finish line and received my medal of completion, I broke into tears. This time I cried tears of joy. At the end of the race, every area of my body ached. But I felt exhilarated. I felt alive. I was a survivor, and completing a half-marathon only fueled me to complete my dissertation.

I still had a long road ahead, yet I knew I could make it. I knew with God's grace and mercy, I could do it. I knew I could do all things through Christ who strengthened me.

04/24/2014

I did it! I ran a half-marathon!!! Wow! I look back in amazement. It was the most wonderful running experience I have had. The weather was perfect. I am so glad I took my camera to take pictures along the route. The memories of that race will last a lifetime. Thank you, God, for the activities of my limbs. Thank you for my legs and the strength of my feet. Thank you for a willing spirit and open mind. Thank you for taking me to the next level to accomplish a goal I never thought was possible. As I prepared for the race a Scripture came to mind, Philippians 6:1. I looked it up and Philippians only goes to chapter 4, so I reversed the numbers... Philippians 1:6 (NIV): "...being confident of this, that He who began a good work in you will carry it on to completion until the day of Christ Jesus."

I finally made my relationship with God a priority, and for the first time in more than 40 years, I experienced pure peace and good love. Once I acknowledged my truth, accepted what went wrong, and owned it, I started to heal. My days of pretending to be okay, when I really wasn't, were gone. I was on a path to give and receive pure, honest, unconditional love. I finally had an opportunity to love myself.

As painful as the divorce was, the pain propelled me to a place of healing from the past and knowing myself on a deeper level. Even before the marriage, I was co-dependent on people, things, or circumstances to make me happy. This dependency mindset caused me to have a victim mentality. Dependency made me desperate. But this time, I became desperate for God. Divorce caused me to realize many things. Because not only did divorce divide my marriage, divorce also divided all the people who were in my life at that point. Folks who had been in my life, for most of my life, fell by the wayside. Any opportunity to be around my family after Mama's death, I was guarded, unable to trust and truly be around any of them without anxiety.

Yet, some family members decided to maintain an active relationship with my ex-husband, which only pushed me to put healthy boundaries around my mental health and well-being. I learned to love everyone from a distance; this included Cookie. I learned to honor and respect her. I learned to forgive her. I also learned to accept what I could not change. I learned to pray for all of my family with the intention of sending love, light, and peace. I was on a mission to move forward. Therefore, my divorce was the death of several relationships, but this life-changing event also gave me new life and new relationships. This divorce helped me set new goals and have a renewed vision — to love and take care of me.

I was grateful for the pain felt and each tear shed because this allowed me to experience God's love more fully. Every single time I felt overwhelmed, He covered me with His grace and mercy. After a while, my faith and perseverance paid off because in August 2015, six years after I had enrolled, I completed my Doctor of Education degree with a focus on Higher Education and Adult Learning from Walden University.

My children, friends, and aunt attended the spring 2016 commencement. Following the ceremony, I found my way through the crowd until I reached my children; I saw their faces and immediately started shouting and praising God. All the hard work and late nights had paid off — I had accomplished my goal and achieved my doctoral degree. Then I saw my aunt, and we immediately embraced each other. While we hugged, it was as if my entire life flashed in my mind like a slide show. I cried for the joy that I stood in. I cried for the generation that carried me. I cried for the future that was brighter than anything I could have ever imagined. It was like forty years of tears were finally released, and I was free to create the life that I wanted.

Life. Death. Life. This best described the cycle of transitions and transformations I found myself in as I stepped out of the old way of thinking and started to adopt a new way to act and think. I had a fresh insight. But in order to step out of the old and cross over into the new, I had to grieve. So many loved ones I lost along my life's journey forced me to grieve, but I had avoided grieving for myself. Now, I had to do the work and acknowledge my truth. . . . I had to own my truth.

01/16/2015
Every day is a struggle. Not a physical struggle, but a mental struggle. Lord, thank you for transforming my fear into confident trust. Thank you for being right by my side each and every day of my life. Lord, I love you. Lord, I thank you. It's been a hard fact to face but my ex-husband is not a good person. Although I married him, built a life with him and had two children with him, that does not make him a good person. And not a good person for me. I also realized that he did not cheat on me because you can't cheat on someone you were never committed to. And he was never committed to me the way that I needed him to be.

I was in denial for many years about this reality. This denial was my own doing; I did not want to see the truth because if I admitted how bad things were and I married him, what did that make me? Well, the truth is revealed, and I cannot . . . will not own his wrongdoings anymore.

I made the decision to leave. I left, but I had to leave so that I could live. I had to leave so my children could live and experience a happy, loving, harmonious life. Something I was told over and over was not possible. Something I was led to believe was a fantasy, a fairy tale. I accepted the things that were told to me because I was with someone incapable of giving it, believing it, and living it. I had to leave so I could finally live.

Yes, it is a daily struggle to undo years of toxic living and toxic thoughts, but the devil is a liar, and I know without a doubt that God has something in store for me. It is my hope that one day my children will realize the courage it has taken me to stand up for what I know is right. I want them to know that the same bloodline of courage that runs through me runs through them. I want them to know that they are worthy of great things and that they are a gift to the world. I want them to know that they are enough.

I had to give myself permission to cry, kick, and scream. I had to give myself permission to go through that hard place I avoided for many years. I had to give myself space and time. I had to honor myself, appreciate my past and get a vision of what was yet to come. It took courage to face my pain. It took strength to examine my mess. And it took supernatural faith to move forward to all that was good with renewed hope, faith, and energy.

The more I avoided grieving for the old me that had to die, the more grief had a grip on me, as if grief stood behind the door, only to grab me from behind and twist my arm as soon as I walked in. I had gone through most of my life in pain, still able to function, yet with limited capacity. No matter how many twists or how severe the pain, I still managed to move — not even realizing that untreated pain in one area created more pain in other areas. For more than forty years, I normalized my pain.

Although I appeared physically able, my emotional health was not good. However, grief has a partner named "joy," and once I had passed through all the lows, joy was on the other side, waiting with open arms and ready to nurse me to new life. Each experience has taught me valuable life lessons:

- I learned to get into complete alignment with my feelings.

- I learned to establish healthy boundaries.

- I learned to love from a distance.

- I learned that every relationship that ended opened an opportunity for new relationships to grow.

- I learned to pray (and plank).

- I learned to have a vision for my life even if I could not see my way through a situation.

- I learned to move toward my goal by putting one foot in front of the other.

- I learned that self-love was not selfish; it was necessary for growth and transformation.

Ultimately, I learned that I am enough. I also learned that alignment, transparency, and clarity were imperative for me to remain whole and move forward because there was an opportunity to grow and grow more with each experience.

But those lessons did not come easy, and they did not come without a struggle. Meanwhile, growth was all about the struggle . . . and the struggle led me to *all that is good.*

> And in the same way – by our faith – the Holy Spirit helps us with our daily problems and in our praying. For we don't even know what we should pray for, nor how to pray as we should; but the Holy Spirit prays for us with such feeling that it cannot be expressed in words. And the Father who knows all hearts knows, of course, what the Spirit is saying as he pleads for us in harmony with God's own will. And we know that all that happens to us is working for our good if we love God and are fitting into his plans. –Romans 8:26-28

About the Author

Dr. James-Etta Goodloe Reed had a stable home life even if she did not have an ideal upbringing. Her great-grandparents, who she affectionately called Mama and Daddy, took care of her in a multi-generational household in rural Kentucky. James-Etta's faith in her family was tested after Mama passed away. Still, she attributes that experience as the catalyst for her determination to overcome every obstacle life put in her way.

Meanwhile, as a young student, she never believed she could attend college, let alone graduate with a degree. Through the encouragement of a good friend, she enrolled and earned an Associate of Arts degree from Western Kentucky University. This experience planted the seed to continue her education to the doctoral level. She understood that when she set out to complete a goal, she had to overcome the obstacle that came with it, no matter what.

James-Etta started running in 2012, the same year she filed for divorce, while she parented two children and wrote her doctoral dissertation. Each life-changing event enabled her to put one foot in front of the other and move forward to all that is good. Now she is encouraging others to do the same: Be strong. Be brave. Do the Work!

To learn more, visit drjamesetta.com. Send inquiries and comments to info@drjamesetta.com.

Scan QR Code
or visit www.padlet.com/dr_jamesetta/allthatisgood
for Bonus Material and Discussion Guide: